Advance Praise for
It's Not Rocket Science!:
Designing Meaningful Learning
Experiences in the Elementary Classroom

"In *It's Not Rocket Science! Designing Meaningful Learning Experiences in the Elementary Classroom* Robert Blake and Lisa Trattner pare down the planning process to five central questions that need to be internalized by teachers, educational leaders, all who engage in the educational process, even including students. Far too much is wasted by the drudgery of requiring educators to pursue endless hours of writing lesson plans, only to find that they don't meet the ever-changing needs of educational situations. Like living a good philosophy of life, embodying these questions nourishes seeds of imagination and improvisation that enrich teaching and learning moment by moment by enhancing the meaning that students experience. Although it may not be as technically sophisticated as rocket science, it may be more important. It collaboratively reconstructs the next (and hopefully better) generations of human beings!"
—William H. Schubert. Professor Emeritus of Curriculum and Instruction, and Former University Scholar, University of Illinois Chicago; Fellow of The International Academy of Education; recipient of the Lifetime Achievement Award in Curriculum Studies of the American Educational Research Association, former President of the John Dewey Society, the Society of Professors of Education, and the Society for the Study of Curriculum History; author of *Love, Justice, and Education,* co-editor of *The Oxford Encyclopedia of Curriculum Studies* (with Ming Fang He), and more than 25 books and 250 articles and chapters.

"*It's Not Rocket Science! Designing Meaningful Learning Experiences in the Elementary* is a straight-forward, practical guide on how student teachers, novice teachers and veteran teachers can engage students in meaningful learning experiences across elementary grade levels and multiple curricular areas. This hands-on resource is a must have in teacher preparation programs, to help facilitate the skills, knowledge and attitudes needed for effective teaching. At the heart of this book, Dr. Blake and Dr. Trattner closely examine five essential questions which primarily ask, "What do I want my students to know? What do I want my students to do?" The authors also explicitly address effective planning, delivery of instruction and how to incorporate a variety of assessments for students, the components required for any successful classroom."

—Linda Miller, M.Ed.
Lecturer III and PDS Supervisor, Department of Elementary Education, Towson University, Towson, Maryland

It's Not Rocket Science!

Critical Literacies and Language: Pedagogies of Social Justice

Series Editors
Brett Elizabeth Blake and Judith M. Dunkerly
Vol. 2

Robert W. Blake, Jr. and Lisa R. Trattner

It's Not Rocket Science!

Designing Meaningful Learning
Experiences in the Elementary Classroom

Foreword by Daniel Ness

PETER LANG
New York · Berlin · Bruxelles · Chennai · Lausanne · Oxford

Library of Congress Cataloging-in-Publication Control Number: 2024031396

Bibliographic information published by the Deutsche Nationalbibliothek.
The German National Library lists this publication in the German
National Bibliography; detailed bibliographic data is available
on the Internet at http://dnb.d-nb.de.

Cover design by Peter Lang Group AG

ISSN 2993-9488 (print)
ISBN 9781636677095 (paperback)
ISBN 9781636677071 (ebook)
ISBN 9781636677088 (epub)
DOI 10.3726/b22128

© 2025 Peter Lang Group AG, Lausanne
Published by Peter Lang Publishing Inc., New York, USA
info@peterlang.com - www.peterlang.com

All rights reserved.
All parts of this publication are protected by copyright.
Any utilization outside the strict limits of the copyright law, without the permission of the
publisher, is forbidden and liable to prosecution.

This applies in particular to reproductions, translations, microfilming, and storage and
processing in electronic retrieval systems.

This publication has been peer reviewed.

To our parents
Robert and Carol (RWB)
And
Stan and Joyce (LRT)

CONTENTS

List of Figures	ix
List of Tables	xi
Acknowledgment	xiii
Foreword	xv
Introduction	1
Chapter 1 Step 1: The Deconstruction	13
Chapter 2 Step 2: The Reconstruction	29
Chapter 3 Step 3: Planning	51
Chapter 4 Assessing Student Learning	71
Index	103
About the Authors	105

LIST OF FIGURES

Figure I.1	Triangle Model of Deconstruction Process	6
Figure I.2	Grade 2 Mathematics Deconstruction	7
Figure I.3	States of Matter: Big Idea and Sub-Topics	7
Figure 1.1	A Template of the Initial Deconstruction Process	15
Figure 1.2	Crafting Sub-topics from the Big Idea	16
Figure 1.3	Content and Process Skills for Moths and Butterflies	17
Figure 1.4	Draft Deconstruction for Moths and Butterflies	19
Figure 1.5	Deconstruction of Second- and Third-Grade Math Topics	20
Figure 1.6	Grade 5 Math Deconstruction	21
Figure 1.7	First-Grade Geography Deconstruction	22
Figure 1.8	Deconstructing the Book *Ramona Forever*	23
Figure 1.9	A Complete Deconstruction Map About the Chesapeake Bay	24
Figure 2.1	A Reconstruction from the Deconstruction	30
Figure 2.2	Original and Revised Taxonomy (Adapted from ©Wilson, Leslie O., 2001)	31
Figure 2.3	Kathlyn's Deconstruction of the Big Idea, The Chesapeake Bay	35
Figure 2.4	Kathlyn's Reconstruction with Written Objectives	37

LIST OF FIGURES

Figure 3.1	Sample. Gradual Release of Responsibility Instructional Lesson Plan	59
Figure 3.2	A Comparison of the Three Part and the 5E Constructivist Learning Model (Also called the *Learning Cycle*)	67
Figure 4.1	Assessment Sequence	75
Figure 4.2	Generating Assessment Ideas for a Unit (Adopted from Wiggins and McTighe, 2005)	77
Figure 4.3	Sample of Unit Assessment Ideas for Unit: Creating New Words	77
Figure 4.4	Holistic Rubric for Expository Writing	80
Figure 4.5	Seventh Grade Holistic Science Rubric	81
Figure 4.6	TIMS Third Grade Multi-Dimensional Mathematics Rubric	84
Figure 4.7	Rubric for a Well-Developed Paragraph with Supported Details	85
Figure 4.8	Carrot Project Student Work. Before Rubric Introduction	86
Figure 4.9	Carrot Project Student Work. After Rubric Introduction	88
Figure 4.10	Unit Assessment Summary Table for Unit on Chesapeake Bay	96
Figure 4.11	Carrot Project Student Sample Number One	101
Figure 4.12	Carrot Project Student Sample Number Two	101

LIST OF TABLES

Table I.1	Sample Process Skills for Science and Language Arts	8
Table 1.1	A Step-by-Step *Deconstruction* Sequence	14
Table 1.2	Student *KNOW* and *DO* statements?	18
Table 2.1	Sample of Action Words (AW) from Bloom's Taxonomy (1956)	32
Table 2.2	Why Write Educational Objectives?	33
Table 2.3	Writing Objectives. A General Process	34
Table 2.4	Purpose of Driving (Essential) Questions. http://grantwiggins.wordpress.com/2013/02/08/on-genuine-vs-bogus-inquiry-using-eqs-properly/	40
Table 2.5	The Difference Between a Driving Question and a Non-driving Question	40
Table 2.6	Overarching Versus Topical Driving Questions	41
Table 2.7	Process Skills as Listed by Padilla (1990). See *Research Matters* #9004. https://narst.org/research-matters/science-process-skills)	43
Table 2.8	A Complete Scope and Sequence from the Chesapeake Bay Deconstruction and Reconstruction	44
Table 3.1	Sample *Chunking* with Timing Within a Lesson	53

Table 3.2	Interactive Strategies for Lessons	54
Table 3.3	Gradual Release Model with General Descriptors of the Instructional Sequence	57
Table 3.4	A Modified Template of a Constructivist Learning Model Framework for Science	64
Table 3.5	Sample CLM Lesson Plan on Survival of the Fittest Lesson	65
Table 4.1	Formative and Summative Multiple Means of Assessments	74
Table 4.2	Multi-Dimensional in Mathematical Problem-Solving	83
Table 4.3	Multi-Dimensional Rubric for ELA Paragraph Writing	83
Table 4.4	TIMS Multi-Dimensional Mathematics Rubric in "Kids" Language	87
Table 4.5	Basic Steps for Creating a Rubric—Pre-Task	90
Table 4.6	Basic Steps for Using and Revising the Rubric—Post-Task	90
Table 4.7	Unit Assessment Summary Table	93
Table 4.8	Pre-Service Interns' Unit Assessment Summary Table of Space Unit	94
Table 4.9	Multi-Dimensional Rubric Profile of Student Work	98

ACKNOWLEDGMENT

We fundamentally believe that the design process, while not easy, should not be as complicated as it is often presented in lengthy curriculum guides. While our intent is not to disparage the manuals crafted by others, we do think a simplified process lends itself to better teacher accessibility in crafting meaningful learning. Curriculum design does not have to be a belabored and a tedious task, but can be simplified, allowing teachers more time to spend on the facilitation of instruction.

This book. This tiny little manual has been mentally crafted over a 30-plus year span of teaching and learning at all levels of the academy. It is difficult to acknowledge all who have impacted us, but in those years, we have had the glorious pleasure of having been influenced by hundreds of teachers, preservice interns, and children, as well as the "giants" we list in the introduction (Dewey, Bruner, Erickson, Gardner, Karplus, McTighe, Schubert, Sizer, Thier, Wiggins, and Yager, to name a few). Each group, in their own way, have significantly transformed our thinking about teaching and learning, and particularly of how we view curriculum design.

We would also be remiss, however, if we did not acknowledge, and thank those who are closer to us, those specific persons who have been supportive, and tolerant, of our idiosyncratic nature of teaching. We owe a debt of gratitude to our big sisters, Brett Elizabeth Blake (Robert) and Jane Lichter (Lisa). Both have been unwavering sounding boards and have greatly supported us through this endeavor.

We greatly thank Linda Miller, our beloved colleague, and an exceptional teacher in her own right, for not only her input and feedback, but for her complete copy-editing of a draft! YOU ROCK!

To our children Matthew and Mackenzie Blake; Carly, Eric and Amanda Trattner who have unknowingly taught us and assisted us in learning *how* to teach all the while, keeping us "real."

Finally, to our spouses, Jennifer Blake and Bradley Trattner, What can we say? We love you and thank you for always being there.

FOREWORD

Daniel Ness
St. John's University

A simple search of a book catalog of any education publisher will undoubtedly yield a plethora of texts on the topic of instruction at the elementary school level—particularly those explaining the "how-to's" for pre-service teachers. But it's only once in a generation, perhaps in a lifetime for that matter, that one comes across a text that sublimely demonstrates the ways in which pre- and in-service teachers can implement best-practice techniques, but successful strategies that are both tried-and-true and engaging for students when considering the developed and structured curriculum. One such book is Ralph Tyler's 1949 locus classicus entitled *Basic Principles of Curriculum and Instruction*, published by the University of Chicago Press. In the present day, another book of this kind is Robert Blake and Lisa Trattner's new publication, *It's Not Rocket Science! Designing Meaningful Learning Experiences in the Elementary Classroom*. To be sure, I am honored to be a part of this book's publication as the author of its foreword.

Another aspect that makes a book immensely influential is the way in which an author takes a seemingly easy-to-understand objective that has few, if any, answers and finds answers to important questions in a convincing and compelling manner. In a prior generation, the famous mathematician and mathematics educator George Pólya, from Stanford University, did just that—he took a burning issue in mathematics, namely, methods of problem-solving, and developed a tested and sound four-step method for solving mathematical problems. So too do Blake and Trattner take an important topic and make it understandable for a wide readership of pre- and in-service teachers, parents, and education researchers; their topic though has to do with best-practice instructional methods that have been proven to work. As they state in their introduction, "... we have found that we often *over* complicate the [lesson] planning process, especially for pre-service teachers ..." They go on to argue that the lesson planning process "... is simply too much writing, too many categories to think about which simply takes away from the central focus of high quality, engaging learning ..." I couldn't agree more. In this treacherous age of audit culture, all too often, the corporate educational establishment continues to usurp authority and autonomy from teachers and students—the two primary constituents that make up the pre-K-12 school population.

Blake and Trattner build their foundation of designing expressive and consequential learning experiences on five key questions that every teacher should be asking when planning lessons for student success: What do I want the students to know?; What do I want our students to do?; Why am I teaching this?; Why am I teaching IT this way?; and How will I know they have learned it? The first two questions are based on curriculum considerations, the second two on instruction, and the fifth, and last question, on assessment.

What makes Blake and Trattner's approach all the more far-reaching is its focus on eliminating mindless, rote, and time-consuming and procedural tasks that only take time away from students' motivation and interest. By simplifying procedural tasks, their technique provides pre- and in-service teachers with the tools they need to make learning a more insightful, inspiring, and intellectual endeavor.

Their overarching philosophy is of the mind that all students—not just those from affluent households—should have the opportunities to engage in enriching activities that will allow the educational system to level the playing field for underprivileged and traditionally marginalized student populations. As part of their technique, Blake and Trattner developed a four-step curriculum process that will equip pre- and in-service teachers with the necessary elements needed to answer the five critical questions outlined above. These chronological steps are (1) deconstructing (analyzing and identifying the big idea), (2) reconstructing (restructuring the big idea with more detail and elaboration), (3) planning (development of instructional techniques to fit each individual student's lived experiences), and (4) assessing (identifying the areas in which individual students need improvement).

Blake and Trattner's interpretation on planning and assessment challenges the corporate, standardized, and one-size-fits-all viewpoint that lessons must be tailored to a monolithic student body and that evaluating students' classwork must be a norm-referenced endeavor that fails to account for each individual student's histories and personal experiences. On the contrary, they construe planning as a teacher's activity "where we organize and structure what we have created into meaningful learning experiences for the students."

Reading Blake and Trattner's book made me realize its vast potential as a blockbuster in the area of instructional methods. It is more than simply a thoughtful, motivating "how-to" for pre- and in-service teachers: It is a sorely overdue text that at once simplifies the byzantine and convoluted nature of the overwhelming majority of lesson planning and assessment books and periodicals and provides a robust overview that takes into consideration the seriousness of planning lessons and evaluating students' work for the primary goal of student success. *It's Not Rocket Science! Designing Meaningful Learning Experiences in the Elementary Classroom* should be required reading for all students and veteran teachers as well as researchers of curriculum and instruction.

Daniel Ness, Professor
Department of Curriculum & Instruction
St. John's University

References

Pólya, G. (2004). *How to solve it: A new aspect of mathematical method*. Princeton University Press.
Tyler, R. (1949). *Basic principles of curriculum and instruction*. University of Chicago Press.

INTRODUCTION

Driving Question

How can we engage students in meaningful learning?

Why This?

This book is a culmination of over thirty years of teaching and learning in all levels of the academy (early childhood, elementary, middle-school, high-school, and higher education), and has one primary purpose; to help pre-service and in-service teachers plan more meaningful and engaging lessons. From these experiences we have found that we often *over* complicate the planning process, especially for pre-service teachers. We are not saying that the many boxes and categories in a lesson plan form that teachers complete are unimportant. What we do contend, however, is that many times it is simply too much writing, too many categories to think about which simply takes away from the central focus of high-quality, engaging learning. We certainly know that there is no substitute for teacher content knowledge, but that does not guarantee good teaching. We concur with Yager and Lutz (1994), who close to thirty years ago stated: "To improve student learning, it will be necessary to focus on a change in teaching.... *How we teach* is more vital that *what we teach!*" (p. 344, emphasis theirs). We believe that the *HOW* of what we do makes *the* difference in learning.

To begin, we always start with five simple questions that are centered around making decisions about the content and processes we want students to gain from the learning, the instructional model used, and how we can assess student understanding. Categorized in this manner, the five questions are (throughout the book we will use the first-person point of view when showcasing these questions):

The Content and Process Skills embedded in the topic.

   (1) *What do I want the students to know?*
   (2) *What do I want our students to do?*

The Instructional Model used for Teaching.

   (3) *Why am I teaching this?*
   (4) *Why am I teaching IT this way?*

Assessing Student Learning.

   (5) *How will I know they have learned it?*

If we can answer each question with a clear educational purpose, then we are good. If we cannot, we need to rethink what we are doing. Based on our experience, one thing we have learned is that planning engaging and meaningful lessons is key to good teaching but also, at times, a daunting and time-consuming task. We believe that our curriculum approach, detailed in this book, provides a concrete attainable method to create better lessons in which students are more directly involved in their learning. While we would like to rely on well-structured and crafted curricula given to us by our schools (department heads or administrators), frequently we cannot. If we are given lesson plans or curricula, it may be scripted, paper-and-pencil, fill-in-the-blank kind of learning, many times meant to teacher-proof the teaching/learning process. In fact, we recall one time (as a first-year teacher) being handed a textbook and told, "Here you go."

Through all these experiences, we have found that there are in fact two distinct audiences for our curriculum approach: pre-service and in-service teachers. As college professors we have worked with undergraduate and graduate students for years who struggle with creating effective learning experience.

We needed to find a way to simplify the process while helping them to have a critical eye for curriculum design. Thus, this method was engendered to provide them with the resources and the understanding needed to be successful. In addition, we have had the chance to work with in-service teachers who are often burdened with the many tasks of educators. They have found that our approach greatly simplifies their work and makes the curriculum more valuable. We have tested and tweaked, and then tested and tweaked some more, in a constantly evolving process. Not only will teachers be able to create meaningful learning, but also learn to understand the nuances involved in curriculum design.

We have also learned through our work with teachers that it is crucial to think of ourselves as professionals, as *faculty*; those members of a professional community; a learned profession (as opposed to the definition of *staff— A group of assistants to a manager . . .*; The American Heritage Dictionary of the English Language, 2022). As faculty, it is incumbent upon us to make professional decisions as to how and what we teach, to have a critical eye on the material (curriculum) given to us by others, and to make decisions, and research, when necessary, the topics we intend to teach (Contrary to what our students think, we do not know everything).

We also need to examine the inequalities and imbalances existing in our schools as our education system is a microcosm of society. It is evident that marginalized students have not consistently been afforded the same opportunities as other students in our schools. This lack of opportunities perpetuates a cycle of injustices and inequities ultimately resulting in disparities in our society. Our goal in teaching is to counter Oakes' (1985, 2005)) timeless findings that lower-track kids, often those of low socio-economic (SES) status or of minority backgrounds are disproportionately given low-level learning experiences (worksheets and/or direct instruction/cookbook activities). Curriculum, as a whole and within disciplines, needs to include truths about all communities and "address myths of origins of various cultures" (Ladson-Billings, 2021, p. 73). We want all students, regardless of background, to have equal access to highly engaging learning experiences.

Why This Way?

In presenting our process we invoke the old saying, *the reason we can see for miles is we stand on the shoulders of giants.* Meaning, we fully admit that many of the fundamental principles we rely on have been around for years, and in reality, that is okay. We believe, however, that our structure, the HOW of what we do, is what makes our process different and accessible to teachers. Thus, as with any good scholars we are forthright with our biases, or as asked in the movie The Commitments, (Parker 1991), "Who are your influences?" These are showcased below.

In 1984 Theodore Sizer founded the Coalition of Essential Schools which began a thirty-three-year endeavor of rethinking teaching and learning. These core ideas of Sizer (1984) have been influential in teaching the fundamentals of learning. Of Sizer's (1984) nine principles, the two that resonate the most here are *Less is more* and *Student as worker*. Working with Sizer at that time was Grant Wiggins who later teamed with Jay McTighe and co-constructed the *Understanding by Design* (UbD) process of curriculum design (Wiggins & McTighe, 1998). Along with fundamental ideas from the Essentials Schools (such as the *Essential Question* and *Exhibition of Mastery*) another idea we lean on from UbD is the notion of *backward mapping*. While we do not begin with the actual assessment in mind, which is often considered the end product of the learning process, we do ask ourselves what it is we want the students to *know* and *do* by the end of the lesson and/or unit.

As we began to think about the planning process through a lens of the *big idea* we also came across Erikson's book (1998), which focuses on *conceptual-based curriculum planning* and how beginning with the overall topic helps to *funnel* or *get at* what we really wanted students to *know* and *do*. Or course, we would be remiss if we did not mention the impact that John Dewey (1910, 1938), Jerome Burner (1960) and William Schubert (1986) have played in our thinking and conceptualization of this process of planning. Simply looking at Bruner's (1960) structure of the subject matter, you will see his impact.

When it comes to instructional models, the intent of this book is to simplify teacher choices. From our experience, the *Gradual Release of Responsibility* (GRR) (Pearson & Gallagher, 1983) and the *Constructivist Learning Model* (CLM) (BSCS, 1989, 1992; Karplus & Thier, 1967; Yager, 1991) are the ones most often used in teaching, particularly with pre-service programs and in our opinion the ones easily accessible to teachers. Each of these models will be presented in more detail in Chapter 3.

The Basic Framework

Defining Our Terms and the General Process

Edwards and Mercer (1987, 2013) articulated that one of the keys to communication is the construction of *common knowledge* where people working together must have a shared understanding of terms and definitions. In arguing against the "culture of power" and criticizing the implied nature of access this power has in schools, Delpit (1988) argued for an explicit approach to instruction, where rules, behaviors, and for us, terminology, need to be presented and shared upfront so that all involved have equal access, ensuring equity in learning.

In this section, we will present and define each term we will use throughout our planning process. These terms will also be reiterated throughout the text. We begin with the *Big Idea/Overarching Concept*[1] and funnel down to the *Sub*-topics, and then to *content* and *process skills* for each sub-topic. The big idea may be the unit topic or what you intend to teach with the sub-topics being the individual parts that make up the big idea. Finally, the content and process skills are the specific *know* and *do* of the lesson/unit. The *Big Idea, Sub-topics, Content,* and *Process Skills* connect to create a purposeful unit of study.

Triangular Model

Big Idea/Overarching Concept

In *The Process of Education*, Jerome Bruner (1960) talks about a "structure of knowledge" the fundamental principles of a particular discipline and how our goal as teachers should be "giving students an understanding of the *fundamental structure* of whatever subjects we choose to teach" (p. 11, *emphasis added*). Bruner suggests that "the teaching and learning of structure, rather than simply the mastery of facts and techniques, is at the center of the classic problem of transfer" (p. 12). Here Bruner suggests that instead of relying on a "bag-of-tricks" or strict pedagogical approaches that enable us to "get across" some sort of content, teachers must first, understand the basic structure; the big idea and related sub-topics, and second, know explicitly what content and process skills one wishes to focus on as we engage students in learning. Figure I.1 showcases our representation of "getting at" the structure of particular teaching topic. Using an inverted triangle, we simply "funnel" (an idea taken from Spradley (1980) and his work on *Participant Observation*) a *Big Idea* into the *Sub-Topics* that make up the *Big Idea*. For each sub-topic, we then attempt to discern/decide/list the specific *content and process skills* embedded within the larger topic. In doing so we delineate not only the *Sub-topics* of our *Big Idea* but also we can use the *content/process skills* to answer fundamental questions one and two:

(1) What do I want the students to know?
(2) What do I want the students to do?

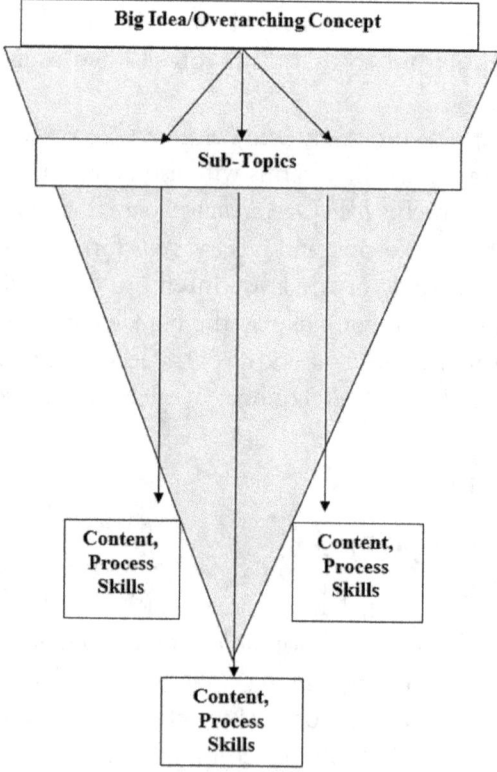

Figure I.1. Triangle Model of Deconstruction Process

Sub-topics

Once a big idea is chosen it can be dissected into fundamental sub-topics. These *sub-topics* are then the individual parts that make up the whole of the big idea. The *Sub-topics* are the individual themes/topics under the big idea.

Figure I.2 provides a pre-service teacher example of the sub-topics that make up the second-grade big idea of measurement (done as an in-class group activity), and Figure I.3 shows an intern's initial set of sub-topics for the states of matter.

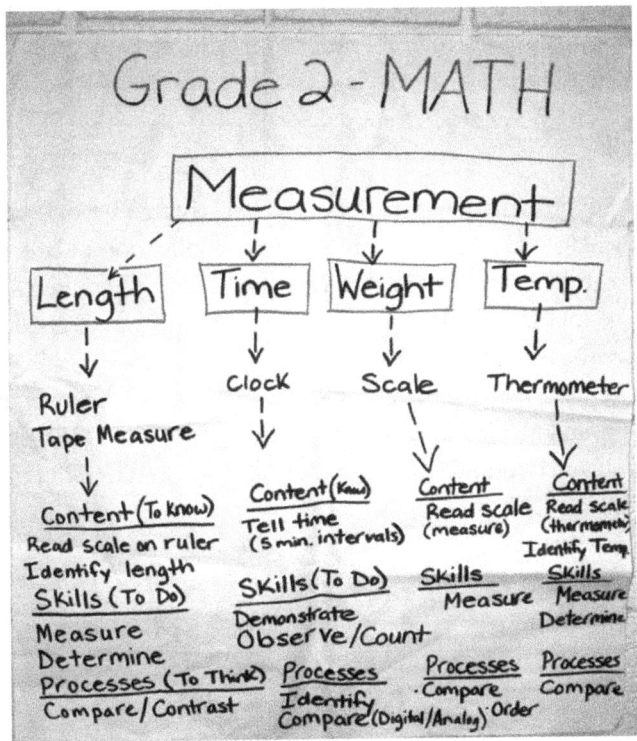

Figure I.2. Grade 2 Mathematics Deconstruction

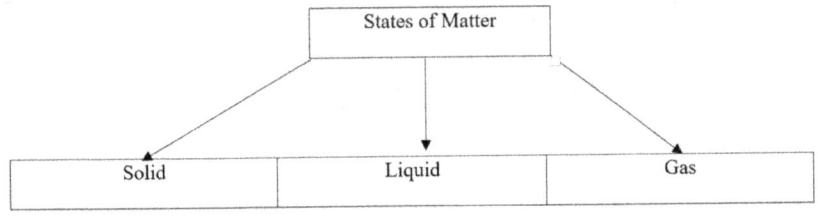

Figure I.3. States of Matter: Big Idea and Sub-Topics

Content

In simple terms, *Content* is the *knowing* of a topic. It includes facts, terms, and definitions of a particular discipline. Many times, simply listing the content knowledge that students will learn is the first-place teachers begin when they decide on a particular topic to teach. Teaching may then be structured to learn this content and testing for content knowledge is the primary means of assessing understanding.

Process Skills

Process Skills are presented as a means of *thinking* that go beyond basic recall of content knowledge. The skills incorporate the application of content and can be a part of the kinesthetic component of teaching. They are used not only to engage students in learning but also to promote an active teaching/learning environment. It is this integration of doing and process skills that is often referred to as *critical thinking*. Examples for both science and language arts process skills are found in Table I.1. Although they are separated in this table, there certainly can be an overlap of the process skills used in different content areas.

Table I.1. Sample Process Skills for Science and Language Arts

Science process skills	Language arts process skills
Observing	Decoding
Classifying	Comprehending
Measuring	Applying
Communicating	Evaluating
Inferring	Remembering
Predicting	Listening
Investigating	Articulating

The Importance of Critical Thinking (CT)

We believe that the major components of the deconstruction model are essential to curriculum design. Specifically, as *Process Skills* are integrated into the model, we go beyond simply creating knowledge through rote memorization and move toward the engagement and application of understanding by students, which we call critical thinking (CT). Defined as "[t]he objective, systematic, and rational analysis and evaluation of factual evidence in order to form a judgement on a subject, issue, etc." (Oxford English Dictionary, 2023), a CT person "... improves the quality of his or her [the student] thinking by skillfully [allowing for] analyzing, assessing, and reconstructing [understanding]" (para 2). Defined this way we believe that conceptually based learning, which our model employs, is central to a CT process.

Current research explores the efficacy of incorporating critical thinking in schools. For example, Alsaleh (2020) comments: "In order to teach CT skills and enable students to master them, teachers should choose a strategy that encourages students to understand and apply such skills" (p. 27). Classroom experiences, therefore, must provide depth of meaning for students to build their cognition, providing ways to move beyond basic content knowledge. Critical thinking is a dynamic process of engaging in information and is rooted in "... knowledge updating, analyzing differences and comparisons, ... observing cause-effect relationships, extracting ideas from examples, ... supporting ideas with examples and evaluating information based on truth value, utility, positive or negative effects" (Florea and Hurjui, 2015, p. 566). In their research on human intelligence, both Flynn (2007) and Nisbett (2009) argue that schools can play a crucial role in honing critical thinking skills, those skills deemed indispensable for success in our increasingly complex world society.

As a result of these studies, it seems clear to us that critical thinking should not only be an integral part of curriculum design, but it must be part of the facilitation of the lesson as it allows students to actively interact with knowledge in a meaningful fashion. We contend that teachers play a vital role in designing learning experiences that move students toward higher order/critical thinking processes and that this deconstruction/reconstruction model provides teachers with the skills and tools to design meaningful learning experiences.

The Basic Structure of the Process

In the following chapters, we will outline our four-step deconstruction/reconstruction process in designing meaningful learning for your students. We repeatedly refer to our five critical questions as we look at each step of our curriculum process.

The Content and Process Skills embedded in the topic.

(1) What do I want the students to know?

(2) What do I want our students to do?

The Instructional Model used for Teaching.

(3) Why am I teaching this?
(4) Why am I teaching IT this way?

Assessing Student Learning.

(5) How will I know they have learned it?

The four steps are:

Step 1—Deconstructing
- Big Idea →Sub-Topics →Content and Process Skills →and Know/Do statements.

Step 2—Reconstructing
- Using know/do statements to write objectives using Bloom taxonomy *action words* (AW) and a *by clause* (BC).
- Scope and sequencing sub-topics into a logical teaching order.
- Crafting *open-ended questions* that help steer the unit and each lesson in a particular direction. (While we call these *driving questions* because they "drive" the lesson and lead to assessments, these types of questions are the same as *Essential Questions* a la, Sizer [1984] and later Wiggins and McTighe [2005]).

Step 3—Planning
- Lesson planning that emphasizes active learning.
  o Essentially responding to the *know* and *do* questions.
- Choosing an instructional model. The two we will showcase are:
  o The *Gradual Release of Responsibility* (GRR) (Pearson & Gallagher, 1983) often used in Language Arts and
  o A *Constructivist Learning Model* (BSCS, 1989, 1992; Karplus & Their, 1967; Yager, 1991) often used in Science

Step 4—Assessing
- Making decisions on HOW students will show understanding both through formative and summative assessments and utilizing both the written objectives and driving questions as foundations to assessments.

Our goal is to provide you with curriculum design framework that challenges your thinking as to how you want to engage your students within the learning process. We believe the sequence is important, but we also know that, as professionals, and as you grow with experience you will find your own way within the process, utilizing what fits you and your students' wants and needs. As we move into our curriculum journey with you in this manual, we start with deconstruction, pulling apart an idea or unit, move to reconstruction, building it back up and then on to the planning stage, where we are creating effective instruction. We end our approach with the assessment phase of curriculum design by outlining the components of assessing students' learning and understandings.

Note

1 The idea of a Concept does equate with the Big Idea and we use both together here. From now on we will simply use the term Big Idea.

References

Alsaleh, N. (2020). Teaching critical thinking skills: Literature review. *TOJET: The Turkish Online Journal of Educational Technology, 19 i.*
American Heritage Dictionary of the English Language, The (5th ed.). (2022). Harper Collins.
Biological Sciences Curriculum Study (BSCS). (1989). *New designs for elementary school science and health*. Dubuque, IA: Kendall Hunt.
Biological Sciences Curriculum Study. (1992). *Science for life and living. Integrating science, technology, and health: Implementation guide.* Kendall/Hunt.
Bruner, J. S. (1960). *The process of education*. Harvard University Press.
Delpit, L.D. (1988). *The Silenced Dialogue: Power and Pedagogy in Educating Other People's Children*. Harvard Educational Review, 58, 280–299.
Dewey, J. (1910). *Science as subject-matter and as method. Science, 31*(787), 121–127.
Dewey, J. (1938). *Experience and education*. Macmillan.
Edwards, D., & Mercer, N. (1987, 2013). *Common knowledge: The development of understanding in the classroom*. London: Routledge.
Flynn, J. R. (2007). *What is intelligence?* Cambridge University Press.
Florea, N. M., & Hurjui, E. (2015). Critical thinking in elementary school children. *Procedia-Social and Behavioral Sciences, 180,* 565–572.
Karplus, R., & Thier, H. D. (1967). *A new look at elementary school science.* Rand McNally University Press.
Ladson-Billings, G. (2021). Culturally Relevant Pedagogy. Asking a Different Question. New York. Teachers College Press.

Nadia, N. M., & Hurjui, E. (2015). Critical thinking in elementary school children. *Proceida Social and Behavioral Sciences, 180*, 565–572.

Nisbett, R. E. (2009). *Intelligence and how to get it. Why schools and culture matter.* W. W. Norton.

Oakes, J. (1985). *Keeping track: How schools structure inequality.* New Haven, CT. Yale University Press.

Oakes, J. (2005). Keeping Track: How Schools Structure Inequality (2nd ed.). New Haven, CT: Yale University Press.

Parker, A. (Director). (1991). *The Commitments.* 20th Century Studios.

Pearson, D. P., & Gallagher, M. C. (1983). The instruction of reading comprehension. Contemporary Educational Psychology. 8(3), 317–344.

Schubert, W. H. (1986). *Curriculum: Perspective, paradigm, and possibility.* New York: Macmillan.

Oxford English Dictionary, The. (2023). Oxford University Press. https://www.oed.com/search/dictionary/?scope=Entries&q=CRITICAL+THINKING

Sizer, T. R. (1984). *Horace's compromise: The dilemma of the American high school.* Houghton Mifflin.

Spradley, J. P. (1980). *Participant observation.* Harcourt Brace Jovanovich.

Wiggins, G., & McTighe, J. (1998). *Understanding by design.* Association for Supervision and Curriculum Development.

Wiggins, G., & McTighe, J. (2005). *Understanding by design* (expanded 2nd ed.). ASCD.

Yager, R. E. (1991). The constructivist learning model: Toward real reform in science education. *The Science Teacher, 58*(6), 52–57.

Yager, R. E., & Lutz, M. V. (1994). Integrated science: The importance of "how" versus "what." *School Science and Mathematics, 94*(7), 338–346.

· 1 ·

STEP 1: THE DECONSTRUCTION

Driving Question

How does breaking-apart the big idea impact meaningful learning?

Deconstructing Your Big Idea

The first step in curriculum design is the *deconstruction*. In order to provide you with the tools to create meaningful learning experiences for your students, we believe that deconstruction is critical to the overall process. Gaining knowledge of the big ideas, content, and process skills embedded within a particular topic is foundational to this first step, and in fact, to teaching. In order to gain that understanding, the deconstruction is THE key piece.

We begin with the *big idea*, or the overarching concept of what we plan to teach. Using the big idea as the foundation, we work through a step-by-step process of figuratively "tearing apart" the main topic into its component sub-topics. From there, we continue the deconstruction and list all content and all process skills believed to be embedded within each sub-topic (The emphasis is on ALL because at this point, we recommend that you do not edit ideas). There may be repetition, particularly with the process skills, but at this stage, it is important to simply create an inclusive list and attend to revising later. Using the content/process skills list, and also referring to your sub-topics, the final step is to write simple, one-sentence statements about what you want students to *know* and *do*. Table 1.1 provides the sequence of steps, and Figure 1.1 shows a generic template to use to guide the deconstruction. Notice that this model (Figure 1.1) has five *Sub-Topics* with each arrow connecting to specific *content* and *process skills* needed for that particular sub-topic. It is important to restate that there may be repetition between and among sub-topics.

Table 1.1. A Step-by-Step *Deconstruction* Sequence

A Step-by-step sequence

(1) BIG IDEA
    a. Look at the curriculum topic and decide on the main idea. (*What are you planning to teach?*)
(2) SUB-TOPICS
    a. Map or web the *Topics* and related *Sub-topics*. (*What parts make up the whole?*)
(3) CONTENT AND PROCESS SKILLS
    a. List what you want them to *know*, which are content skills.
    b. List what they are to do, which are process skills.
(4) *KNOW* and *DO* STATEMENTS
    a. Write specific statements of what you want students to *know* and *do* by end of the lesson.

STEP 1: THE DECONSTRUCTION

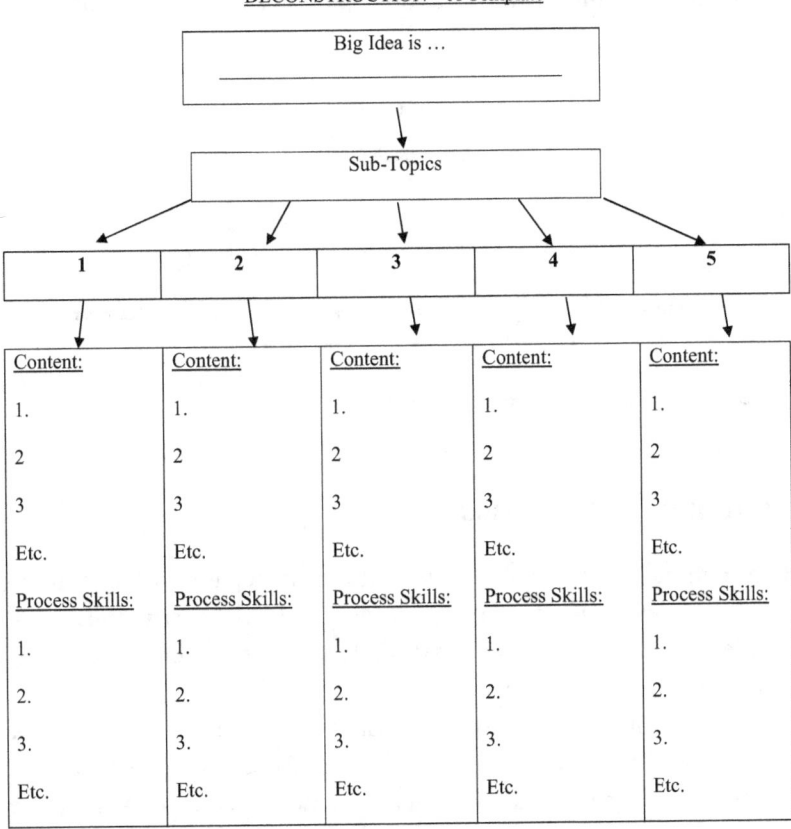

Figure 1.1. A Template of the Initial Deconstruction Process

What will the students be able to KNOW? and DO by the end? *These are simply written statements you think are important.*
1.
2.
3. etc.

Sample Deconstruction

The Big Idea and Sub-topics

The deconstruction process begins with the big idea; using either one from your curriculum or a topic you want to teach. Figure 1.2 shows a deconstruction of moths and butterflies into three sub-topics: *Characteristics, Life Cycle, and Behavior.*

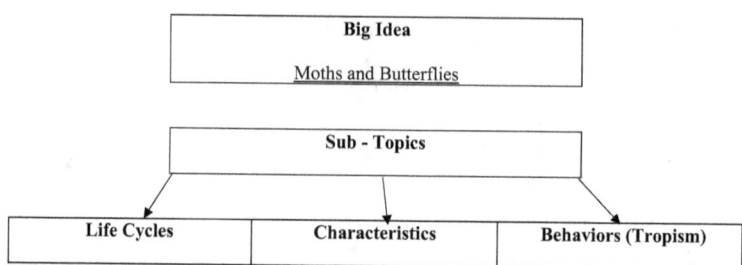

Figure 1.2. Crafting Sub-topics from the Big Idea

Content and Process Skills

Once the general sub-topics are created, the next step is to list all content and process skills relevant to that sub-topic. Ideally, the deconstruction flows from the big idea to the sub-concept, and directly into the content/process skills for *each* sub-concept (Figure 1.3).

It is important to not revise at the onset, but to include every idea that you think relates to the sub-topic. At the beginning, we encourage the completion of only a single strand of thought, or one sub-concept of a big idea but it is important to complete the entire chart for each sub-topic.

STEP 1: THE DECONSTRUCTION 17

Big Idea, Concept, and or Topic:

Moths and Butterflies

Sub-concepts

Characteristics	Life Cycle	Behaviors

Content and Process Skills Embedded in Each Sub-Concept

Content (To Know)	Content (To Know)	Content (To Know)
1. Insects	1. Define complete and incomplete metamorphosis.	1. Reactions to stimuli
2. # of Body Parts	2. Specific stages	2. Interrelationships with plants
Process Skills (Do and Think)	Process Skills (Do and Think)	Process Skills (Do and Think)
1. Observe	1. Observe	1. Design experiment
2. Count	2. Diagram	2. Observe
3. Analyze	3. Compare/Contrast	3. Analyze
4. Compare/contrast		4. Synthesize

Figure 1.3. Content and Process Skills for Moths and Butterflies

Writing Know and Do Statements

Continuing with Moths and Butterflies, the last step is to create a list of sentences of what you think students should *know* and *do* at the end of this learning cycle (Table 1.2). Generate all ideas of content knowledge and process skills you think are important and valuable to learning about moths and butterflies.

Table 1.2. Student *KNOW* and *DO* statements?

1. List the three body parts of an insect.
2. List the number of legs and wings all insects have.
3. Observe preserved and live specimens of insects and verify body structure.
4. Diagram at least three different insects from samples and note similarities and potential differences.
5. Describe what the term "life cycle" means.
6. Compare/contrast the stages of complete and incomplete metamorphosis.
7. Compare and contrast mealworms to earthworms and diagram and explain why one is an insect and the other is not.
8. Raise mealworms and document, by drawing and writing, daily changes of the mealworm in a life cycle.
9. Conduct an experiment that tests a mealworm's behavior toward certain stimuli (like water, heat, light, dark).
10. Investigate, either through direct observation in a garden or via the internet, the relationships between insects and plants.

A Completed Deconstruction

A draft deconstruction of Moth and Butterflies is shown in Figure 1.4. Please note, that this is not THE final product, but only one of many, thus the term, draft. What is included is dependent on you, any potential curricular resources you have, and if you are following any state or national standards. The key is to make sound, professional decisions on what you want the students to ultimately *know* and *do* when studying moths and butterflies. Also note the **bold** words. These are the actions you will expect from students. Later, in Chapter 2, you will see how these words directly relate to those action words (AW) found in any list of Bloom's Taxonomy.

STEP 1: THE DECONSTRUCTION   19

Big Idea, Concept, and or Topic:

Moths and Butterflies

Sub-concepts

Characteristics	Life Cycle	Behavior

Content and Process Skills Embedded in Each Sub-Concept

Content (To Know)	Content (To Know)	Content (To Know)
1. Insects	1. Define complete and incomplete metamorphosis.	1. Reactions to stimuli
2. # of Body Parts	2. Specific stages	2. Interrelationships with plants
Process Skills (Do and Think)	Process Skills (Do and Think)	Process Skills (Do and Think)
1. Observe	1. Observe	1. Design
2. Count	2. Diagram	2. experiment
3. Analyze	3. Compare/Contrast	3. Observe
4. Compare/contrast		4. Analyze
		5. Synthesize

Students will be Able to *KNOW* and *DO* by the end of the lesson?

1. **List** the three body parts of an insect.

2. **List** the number of legs and wings all insects have.

3. **Observe** preserved and live specimens of insects and verify body structure.

4. **Diagram** at least three different insects from samples and describe similarities and potential differences.

5. **Describe** what the term "life cycle" means.

6. **Compare/ contrast** the stages of complete and incomplete metamorphosis.

7. **Compare and contrast** mealworms to earthworms and diagram and explain why one is an insect and the other is not.

9. **Grow** mealworms and **diagram** and **take notes** of daily changes of the mealworm in a life cycle.

10. **Conduct** an experiment that tests a mealworms behavior towards certain stimuli (like water, heat, light, dark).

11. **Investigate,** either through direct observation in a garden or via the internet, the relationships between insects and plants.

Figure 1.4. Draft Deconstruction for Moths and Butterflies

Other Content Deconstructions

The examples which follow are from several other curriculum content areas, other than science. Each is a real deconstruction, created by students in a university methods class. Figure 1.5 shows two mathematic examples for lower elementary grades (created on chart paper and shared with the class). Figure 1.6 represents one for fifth-grade mathematics. Notice that while the content may be different, the process skills and the overall structure are similar.

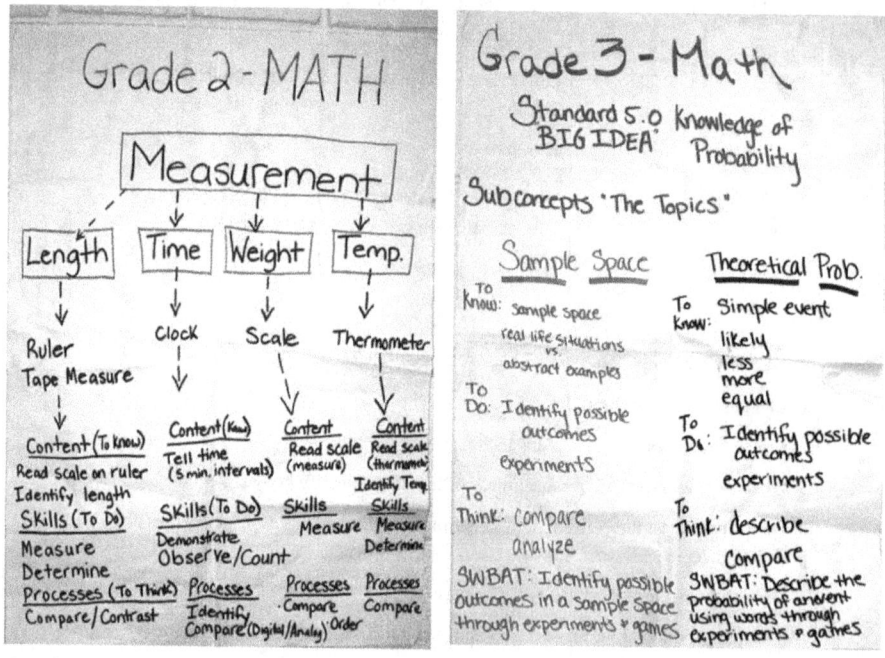

Figure 1.5. Deconstruction of Second- and Third-Grade Math Topics

STEP 1: THE DECONSTRUCTION   21

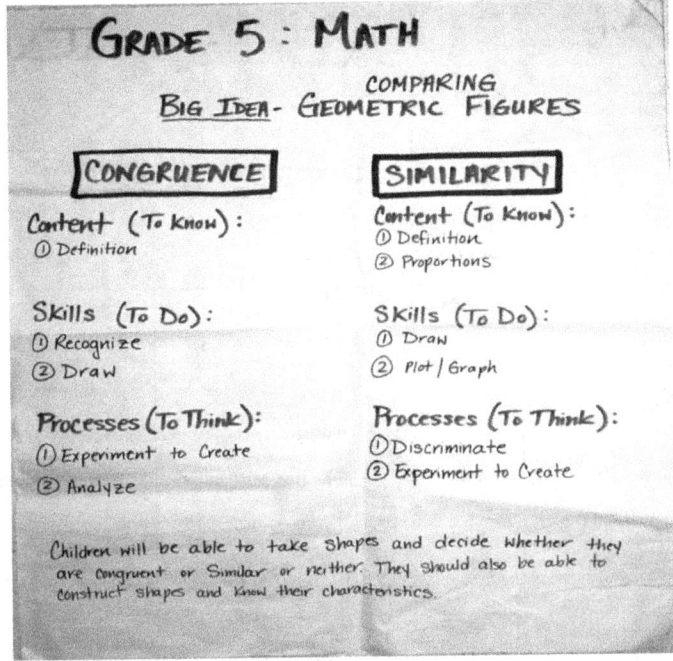

Figure 1.6. Grade 5 Math Deconstruction

Figure 1.7 showcases a first-grade geography deconstruction. While this example may seem beyond the realm of first grade, it provides a solid foundation for the teacher to use in deciding what to teach.

The final two examples are from a third-grade language arts (Figure 1.8) and third-grade science deconstruction (Figure 1.9). We include the language arts example for two reasons. First, the big idea is a theme of a book, which was unique from others, and second, the fact that the intern used the general idea of the template but created her own structure. She included the same parts as described but applied the terms using a novel. Both examples pictured showcase the complete deconstruction model.

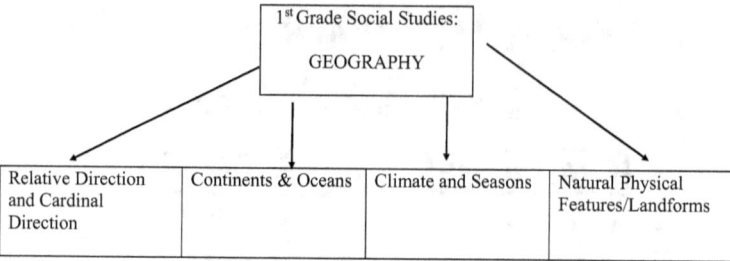

Relative Direction and Cardinal Direction	Continents & Oceans	Climate and Seasons	Natural Physical Features/Landforms
Content: 1. What is relative and cardinal direction? 2. How are they different from one another? 3. Follow relative and cardinal direction.	**Content:** 1. What is a continent? 2. What are the continents? 3. What is an ocean? 4. What are the different oceans? 5. What are the differences between the continents?	**Content:** 1. What is climate? 2. What are the different seasons? 3. How are the different regions of the world affected by the seasons and climates?	**Content:** 1. What are natural physical features/ landforms? 2. How do they differ by region of the world?
<u>Processes Skills</u> 1. Define 2. Label 3. List 4. Illustrate 5. Observe 6. Classify 7. Compare and contrast	<u>Processes Skills</u> 1. Define 2. List 3. Label 4. Observe 5. Classify 6. Compare and contrast	<u>Processes Skills</u> 1. Define 2. Describe 3. Label 4. Investigate 5. Observe 6. Classify 7. Communicate 8. Compare and contrast	<u>Processes Skills</u> 1. Describe 2. Identify 3. Label 4. Illustrate 5. Observe 6. Classify 7. Analyze 8. Compare and contrast

Figure 1.7. First-Grade Geography Deconstruction

STEP 1: THE DECONSTRUCTION

<u>Big Idea</u>
Reading—<u>Ramona Forever</u> by Beverly Cleary
<u>3rd Grade</u>
<u>Sub-Topics</u>

3rd Grade Death Marriage New Sibling Beverly Cleary/Ramona

<u>Content and Process Skills Embedded in Each Sub-Topic</u>

<u>3rd Grade</u>: Discuss, explore and list what they like and dislike about being a 3rd grader.

<u>Death</u>: Reflect, describe and explain the death of Ramona's cat and how you feel about it

<u>Marriage</u>: Act out, dramatize and interpret a wedding scene

<u>New Sibling</u>: Explore, identify and compare who has a sibling in the class and how it feels to be youngest or oldest.

<u>Beverly Cleary/Ramona</u>: Explore, assess and review the author's website.

<u>What should students know and do?</u>

<u>3rd Grade</u>:

1. Students will know/explore about themselves by listing the best and worst things about being in 3rd grade or being a 3rd grader, then post combined results in the classroom.

Death:

1. Students will know that death is a natural process and turn their written reflections into a short story about death, adding illustrations.

Marriage:

1. Students will know what a wedding will look like by acting out marriage scene in story.

New Sibling:

1. Students will know that older or younger siblings are common, and everyone feels differently about them by collecting data from classmates using a questionnaire.

Beverly Cleary/Ramona:

1. Students will know who the author is, how to navigate a website and more about Ramona by exploring Cleary's website.

Figure 1.8. Deconstructing the Book *Ramona Forever*

Sub-Topic Pollution and Human Impact	Sub-Topic Watershed	Sub-Topic Ecosystems and Habitats
Content (Know) 1. Impact on Bay. 2. Point and Non-point pollution. 3. Ways we can help Bay's condition.	**Content (Know)** 1. Define watershed. 2. Chesapeake Bay watershed coverage (states and streams/rivers). 3. Stages of water cycle.	**Content (Know)** 1. Habitats in the Chesapeake Bay watershed. 2. Parts of a food chain (consumers, producers, decomposers). 3. Importance of a balanced food chain.
Process Skills (Do and Think) 1. Observe 2. Predict 3. Define 4. Formulate 5. Communicate 6. Assess 7. Grade 8. Determine 9. Compare	**Process Skills (Do and Think)** 1. Define 2. Predict 3. Observe 4. Communicate 5. Construct 6. Explain 7. Connect 8. Compare	**Process Skills (Do and Think)** 1. Classify 2. Define 3. Design 4. Analyze 5. Compare and Contrast 6. Determine

The Students Will Be Able To

1. Define watershed.
2. Construct a model of a watershed.
3. Predict how water will flow in a watershed model.
4. Observe and communicate how a watershed model works (water goes from high to low).
5. Define and compare the different stages of the water cycle.
6. Define and compare point and non-point source pollutants.
7. Determine how pollutants impact the Chesapeake Bay watershed (positive or negative).

> 8. Predict outcomes of pollution experiments.
> 9. Observe pollution experiments and communicate what they observed.
> 10. Formulate ways in which we can help the condition of the Chesapeake Bay.
> 11. Determine, assess, and grade the "health" of the schoolyard and school stream.
> 12. Observe different components of the school stream.
> 13. Define and classify different organisms by consumer, producer, or decomposer.
> 14. Compare and contrast the different parts of a food chain.
> 15. Recognize and analyze cause-and-effect relationships in the food chain.
> 16. Identify the seven different habitats located in the Chesapeake Bay watershed.
> 17. Design a model of a Chesapeake Bay habitat.
> 18. Determine the relationship between producers and consumers.

Figure 1.9. A Complete Deconstruction Map About the Chesapeake Bay

Onto Reconstruction

The figures above provide concrete and real examples of various content deconstructions. By examining the models, the clarity of the process becomes evident, as well as how meaningful the work is prior, to constructing the unit. As a teacher, if you are unsure of the topic and content within a particular subject, this deconstruction process allows you to tease-out the pieces of the whole (the *sub-topic of a big idea*) and provides the opportunity to generate a list of ALL possible *content* and *process skills* which are embedded within the discipline. Essentially, you are creating your own content primer and from this list, you can then begin to make plans of what you may teach. Certainly, you want to take into consideration the developmental level of your students, any requirements from standards/curriculum, and the amount of time you have to teach a particular topic. This becomes the next step of effective curriculum planning, the *reconstruction* of the unit.

Reconstruction is one that veteran teachers often do intuitively, moving from deconstruction directly into lesson planning. For novice teachers, however, we suggest completing the reconstruction because it provides the opportunity to revise the original list of ideas, but also allows you to work with the sub-topic and content/process skills in a way that enables you to formulate a scope and sequence of what to teach next. As we outline the main components of reconstruction in the next chapter, the distinct process of systematically putting the lesson back together becomes easily assessable.

Chapter 1: Deconstruction Activities

Activity One

- Finish the deconstruction model below for a science unit for 2nd graders. The *big idea* and *sub-topics* have been determined. Add the *content* and *process skills*. Refer to the chapter to see an example.

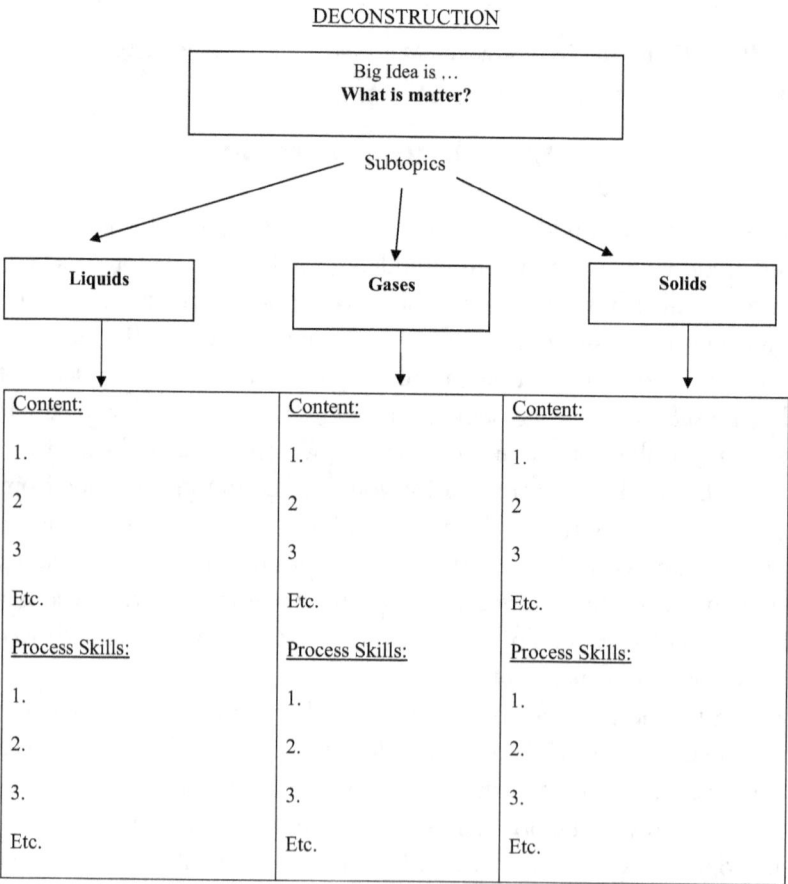

Activity Two

- Pick a topic that you want to teach or one you think you will teach. Using the deconstruction template compete the following:

List the Big Idea or Main Topic

- o Write a succinct one sentence statement of why the big idea is important.
- o List at least one sub-topic.
- o After listing one sub-topic, list ALL specific content embedded within that sub-topic (as many ideas as can think of).
- o For the same sub-topic, list at least two process skills which you think are important.
- o For the same sub-topic, list at least five statements of what students will *know* and *do*.
- o Write one idea on how students will show understanding and WHY this is useful.

Analysis/Cognitive Processing.
Describe how you felt about this deconstruction process. What part(s) helped you the most? How might you apply this to your future planning?

· 2 ·

STEP 2: THE RECONSTRUCTION

Driving Question

How does the reconstruction process impact meaningful learning?

Step 2 is a three-part process in which the *sub-topics* are organized in a logical *scope* and *sequence* (the order in which you plan to teach), and the *know* and *do* statements are fine-tuned into *objectives*, often called learning outcomes. Our sequence is:

(1) *Scope and sequencing* sub-topics into a logical teaching order.
(2) Using *know/do* statements to write objectives using Bloom's taxonomy that contain Action Words (AW) and a By Clause (BC). See section on objective writing later in this chapter.
(3) Crafting *open-ended questions* that help steer the unit and each lesson in a particular direction. While we call these *driving questions* because they "drive" the lesson and lead to assessments, these types of questions are the same as *Essential Questions* à la Sizer (1984) and later Wiggins and McTighe (2005). For our purposes, we will use the term, *Driving Questions*.

Part One: Scope and Sequencing

In this first step in our process, the deconstruction sub-topics are reviewed, discussed (if working in a team), and ordered in a teaching sequence. Each topic could be a separate lesson or multiple lessons with the scope and sequence representing an ideal unit plan. This process is actually quite simple (often completed during the deconstruction) but is also malleable, in that the sequence can change, depending on the needs of the students. Figure 2.1 shows the result of the scope and sequencing process of the sub-topics. Notice that the original sequence did not change (reading left to right) but the students added a driving question (discussed later) for each sub-topic.

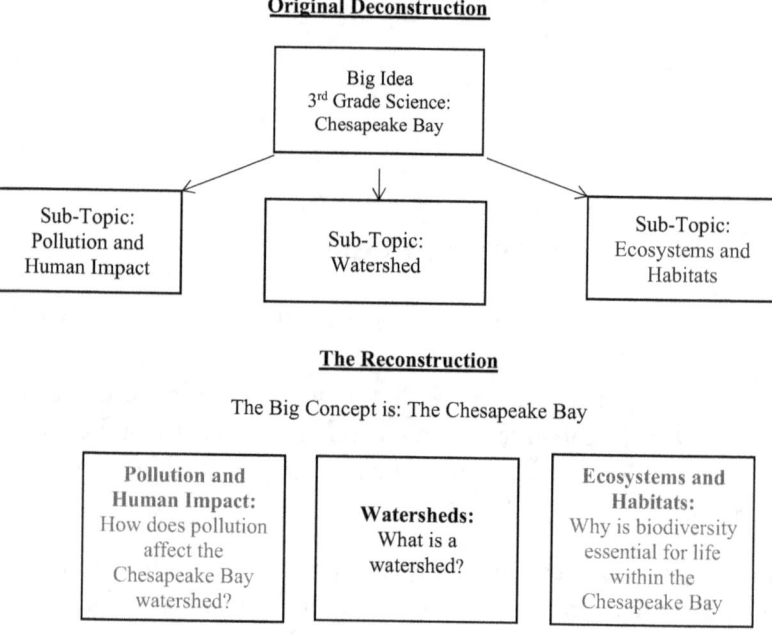

Figure 2.1. A Reconstruction from the Deconstruction

Part Two: Utilizing Bloom's Taxonomy of Educational Objectives

Using Bloom's Taxonomy (1956), we next focus on a method of constructing objectives/learning outcomes that will emphasize the know and do. Since our aim is for active learning, our goal is for objectives that reflect "doing." The original Bloom's Taxonomy of Educational Objectives (1956), which has been part of curriculum design for over sixty years, has since been revised by Anderson and Krathwohl (2001) and referred to as *Bloom Revised*. Sometimes criticized for being used to construct objectives that "measure" discrete bits of knowledge and skills, we maintain that Bloom's taxonomy is essential to the planning process and is especially critical for teachers in training as it helps them to create "higher order" thinking lessons. Using the Bloom's taxonomy, we encourage students to incorporate action words from the higher-level cognitive categories (Analysis, Synthesis, and Evaluation). These process skills are so often championed in current education circles and ones that emphasize more advanced critical thinking. The comparative structure of the original and the revised taxonomy is shown in Figure 2.2 and can be found almost limitlessly on the internet. Much of what we present here will rely on the original, 1956, taxonomy.

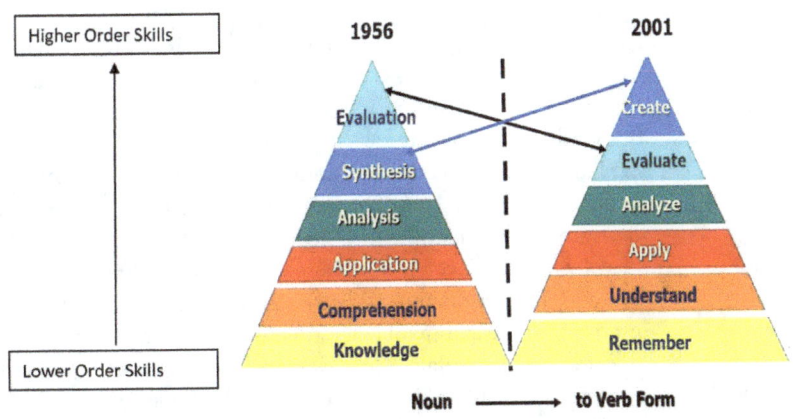

Figure 2.2. Original and Revised Taxonomy (Adapted from ©Wilson, Leslie O., 2001)

In this image (Figure 2.2), the levels are organized with the lowest level of learning representing the bottom, and the more sophisticated levels, or higher-order thinking skills, toward the top. Our emphasis will be on the *Action Words* (AW) listed in each level. In a different representation, one that includes action words (Table 2.1), lower- to higher-level moves from left to right. By simply comparing action words on the far left with those on the far right, we can see that we are asking for greater cognitive thought processes using those on the right (Critical Thinking/Higher-Order Skills). We place substantial prominence on incorporating an action word (AW) into the written objective, and specifically, higher-order action words that necessitate more student engagement in learning.

Table 2.1. Sample of Action Words (AW) from Bloom's Taxonomy (1956)

Lower-order thinking → **Higher-order thinking**

Knowledge	Comprehension	Application	Analysis	Synthesis	Evaluation
Being able to recall learned information.	Being able to change information from one form or format to another.	Being able to use learned information to new situations.	Being able to identify relationships between or among information.	Being able to use information to produce a new or original end product.	Being able to judge its value and create and/or develop something new.
count	classify	apply	analyze	argue	appraise
define	describe	articulate	categorize	assess	adapt
describe	discuss	calculate	compare	assemble	assemble
find	distinguish	change	connect	convince	compose
identify	explain	chart	contrast	critique	construct
label	express	compute	criticize	debate	create
list	illustrate	construct	deduce	defend	design
locate	identify	develop	differentiate	editorialize	develop
match	infer	examine	discriminate	estimate	facilitate
memorize	interpret	experiment	estimate	evaluate	hypothesize
name	locate	explain	evaluate	formulate	invent
outline	order	illustrate	experiment	judge	modify
recall	predict	interpret	infer	justify	negotiate
recite	relate	manipulate	model	persuade	plan
select	report	modify	organize	predict	propose
state	restate	operate	plan	propose	revise
tabulate	summarize	predict	prioritize	rationalize	simulate
tell	transform	produce	question	summarize	support
visualize	translate	solve	test	support	validate

Writing Objectives

Why?

Writing formal objectives provides the opportunity to consciously and systematically articulate the content and process skills that students are to learn during the lesson. Specifically, objectives allow educators to identify what you want the students to be able to *know*, *demonstrate*, or *exhibit* at the end of the lesson (fundamentally, the KNOW and DO of learning). By thinking about *how* students will show understanding you are also beginning to think about the process of constructing assessments. Therefore, objectives and assessments become directly associated with the "how" of your teaching. Objectives can also be sequenced within a topic, from simple to complex, and used across topics to form the basis of a unit plan. Objectives, therefore, need to be carefully crafted, representing the variety of ways in which students learn. Table 2.2 provides a synopsis of why written educational objectives are imperative in designing meaningful learning experiences.

Table 2.2. Why Write Educational Objectives?

1. To be more precise in planning (To plan activities linked directly to objectives),
2. To assist in planning lessons that incorporate higher-order thinking skills,
3. To construct lessons that promote *Application, Analysis, Synthesis, and Evaluation*, and that incorporate *Affective and Psychomotor* Domains,
4. To place objectives into a logical teaching sequence (After deciding goals and task analysis),
5. To create *Assessments and Evaluations* that are consistent with and linked to the objectives, and
6. To incorporate during classroom instruction to keep students, teachers, and administrators aware of the teaching goals.

How?

Our general process for writing objectives is outlined in Table 2.3. While there are four main pieces to this, initially our main focus is on the *Action Word* (AW) and the *By Clause* (BC). While both the *Audience* (A) and the *Degree* (D) are important components (the audience being quite simple, your students), we prefer to first focus on AW and BC because these allow you to clearly emphasize what you want the students to *know/do* and how you want them to do "it."

Table 2.3. Writing Objectives. A General Process

Four Main Parts to an Objective
(A, AW, BC, and D)

1. Who? Your AUDIENCE (A) or your students.
    a. *Third-grade students will be able to . . .*
2. What? The ACTION WORD (AW) is taken from Bloom's Taxonomy. A specific action that allows students to show/do. Always think about simple to complex and moving from lower- to higher-order thinking skills.
    a. *Third-grade students will be able to compare/contrast the elements of fiction and non-fiction writing . . .*
3. How? The BY CLAUSE (BC). Essentially what students will do.
    a. *Third-grade students will be able to compare/contrast the elements of fiction and non-fiction writing by reading one passage each of fiction and non-fiction.*
4. How much? The DEGREE (D) or level of competency. Could be *Correct, 4 out of 5, to within the nearest ¼ inch*, etc. YOU decide on the cutoff level of competency for each object. (This part is often omitted in classroom lesson plans.)
    a. *Third-grade students will be able to compare/contrast two elements of fiction and non-fiction writing by reading one passage of each.*

As mentioned in our discussion of Bloom (1956), lists of taxonomy action words are plentiful on the internet and here we simply provide but one example. For us the most important part of this particular step is to spend time on comparing/contrasting the *lower-order* versus the *higher-order* action words, and then decide how to bring higher-order thinking skills into your teaching. The reason both lower- and higher-order words are important is because doing so leads to more meaningful learning and, we argue, more meaningful assessments (assessing will be discussed in Chapter 4). Even in the 1980s, Bloom (1984, cited in Hart(1994) lamented the fact that teaching as well as assessing were still stuck in lower-level skills, stating:

> Even after the sale of over one million copies of the *Taxonomy of Educational Objectives—Cognitive Domain* and over a quarter of a century of using this domain in preservice and inservice teacher training, still over 95 percent of test questions that U.S. students are now expected to answer deal with little more than information. *Our instructional methods, and our testing methods rarely rise above the lowest category of the taxonomy: knowledge.* (Hart, 1994, p. 43; emphasis added)

STEP 2: THE RECONSTRUCTION

The next set of Figures (2.3 and 2.4) are samples of the process from a complete *Deconstruction* to a *Reconstruction* crafted by the same teacher intern. The key for this section is to see how she linked the KNOW/DO deconstruction statements to the written objectives in her reconstruction.

Deconstruction Map

Big Idea 3rd Grade Science: Chesapeake Bay		
Sub-Topic Pollution and Human Impact	Sub-Topic Watershed	Sub-Topic Ecosystems and Habitats
Content (Know): 1. Impact on Bay. 2. Point and Non-point pollution. 3. Ways we can help Bay's condition.	Content (Know): 1. Define watershed. 2. Chesapeake Bay watershed coverage (states and streams/rivers). 3. Stages of water cycle.	Content (Know): 1. Habitats in the Chesapeake Bay watershed. 2. Parts of a food chain (consumers, producers, decomposers). 3. Importance of a balanced food chain.
Process Skills 1. Observe 2. Predict 3. Define 4. Formulate 5. Communicate 6. Assess 7. Grade 8. Determine 9. Compare	Process Skills 1. Define 2. Predict 3. Observe 4. Communicate 5. Construct 6. Explain 7. Connect 8. Compare	Process Skills 1. Classify 2. Define 3. Design 4. Analyze 5. Compare and Contrast 6. Determine

Continued

The Students Will Be Able to Know and Do: (AW, as indicated Bloom, are *italicized* to show emphasis)

1. *Define* watershed.
2. *Construct* a model of a watershed. *Predict* how water will flow in a watershed model.
3. *Observe* and *communicate* how a watershed model works (water goes from high to low).
4. *Define* and *compare* the different stages of the water cycle.
5. *Define* and *compare* point and non-point source pollutants.
6. *Determine* how pollutants impact the Chesapeake Bay watershed (positive or negative).
7. *Predict* outcomes of pollution experiments.
8. *Observe* pollution experiments and *communicate* what they observed.
9. *Formulate* ways in which we can help conditions of the Chesapeake Bay.
10. *Determine, assess, and grade* the "health" of the schoolyard and school stream.
11. *Observe* different components of the school stream.
12. *Define* and *classify* different organisms by consumer, producer, or decomposer.
13. *Compare* and *contrast* the different parts of a food chain.
14. *Recognize* and *analyze* cause-and-effect relationships in the food chain.
15. *Identify* the seven different habitats located in the Chesapeake Bay watershed.
16. *Design* a model of a Chesapeake Bay habitat.
17. *Determine* the relationship between producers and consumers.

Figure 2.3. Kathlyn's Deconstruction of the Big Idea, The Chesapeake Bay

STEP 2: THE RECONSTRUCTION

Reconstruction Map

The Big Idea
The Chesapeake Bay

Pollution and Human Impact: How does pollution affect the Chesapeake Bay watershed?	Watersheds: What is a watershed?	Ecosystems and Habitats: Why is biodiversity essential for life within the Chesapeake Bay ecosystem?

Objectives

1. Third-grade students will be able to explain how pollution impacts the Chesapeake Bay by reading a text.	1. Third-grade students will be able to create an operational definition for watershed and predict how it relates to the Chesapeake Bay by creating a diagram.	1. Third-grade students will be able to compare and contrast the different parts of a food chain by creating a model of the Chesapeake Bay food chain.
2. Third-grade students will be able to define and compare point and non-point pollutants by participating in a pollution experiment.	2. Third-grade students will be able to predict how the water will flow by constructing a working model of a watershed.	2. Third-grade students will be able to define and classify different animals/plants (that live in the Bay) as producers, decomposers, or consumers by completing a sorting activity.
3. Third-grade students will be able to observe different pollution experiments by observing different scenarios.	3. Third-grade students will be able to observe and explain how a watershed model works (water travels from high to low) by presenting their findings to classmates.	3. Third-grade students will be able to recognize cause-and-effect relationships in the food chain by creating a model.
4. Third-grade students will be able to investigate ways in which we can clean up pollution in the Bay by reading different texts.		4. Third-grade students will be able to identify the seven different habitats located in the Chesapeake Bay watershed by reading a brief article about each.

Continued

Reconstruction Map

5. Third-grade students will be able to observe and assess major factors that influence the "health" of their schoolyard by completing "My Schoolyard Report Card."
6. Third-grade students will be able to observe and record different components of the school stream by completing a stream assessment.
7. Third-grade students will be able to formulate ways to help our Earth by creating an Earth Day poster.

4. Third-grade students will be able to identify which rivers and streams are a part of the Chesapeake Bay watershed by creating a diagram.
5. Third-grade students will be able to define and compare the different stages of the water cycle by creating a water cycle wheel diagram.

5. Third-grade students will be able to model the habitats of the Chesapeake Bay watershed by constructing shoebox dioramas.
6. Third-grade students will be able to demonstrate the relationship between producers and consumers by playing "Oh Deer!"

Figure 2.4. Kathlyn's Reconstruction with Written Objectives

Finally, the samples used show us the direct flow and connection to each part of the process, moving from

Big Idea→ Sub-topics→ Content/Process skills→ Know/Do→ Scope and Sequence→ Objectives.

Again, we have found that savvy teacher interns and veteran teachers move directly from the *KNOW/DO* to *Objectives*, without actually listing the scope and sequence. We maintain, however, that completing this procedure a few times helps to internalize the sequencing of teaching within this process of planning meaningful learning.

Part Three: Crafting Driving Questions

Finally, our goal is to craft at least one open-ended question per lesson that can be used to help guide a lesson's purpose. While we use the term *Driving Questions* (DQ), we again give credit to Sizer (1984) and Wiggins and McTighe (1998) when it comes to the fundamental idea of *Essential Questions* (EQ).[1]

We want teachers to realize that the *know and do* in a learning experience has a direct relationship to the type of questions we ask. If we are interested in content knowledge, or the students' *knowing* and/or *comprehending* something, our questions will generally be *closed-ended*, ones that have a simple yes/no, right/wrong answer. If we are interested in students *analyzing extending, applying, or inferring*, providing responses in their own words and formulating ideas based on their experiences then we most likely ask *open-ended* questions.

Why and how we ask questions goes a long way toward engaging students within a learning process. While important for all students, this is particularly critical for those students thought to be "at risk" or from poor, low socioeconomic backgrounds, students who are often deemed not capable of engaging in higher-level thinking activities (see Oakes, 1985, 2005).

The Purpose of Driving Questions

Driving questions (*essential, inquiry,* or *guiding questions*) are questions that are posed to students at the beginning of a unit and lesson and routinely referred back to throughout the teaching. Thus, they are recursive and timely. Asked in an open-ended format, *driving questions* encourage students to incorporate prior knowledge, pulling from previous experiences and are used at the beginning of a lesson to not only motivate students about a topic but also used by the teacher to assess prior knowledge. Table 2.4 articulates the main purposes of these questions as outlined by Wiggins (2013), and Table 2.5 showcases the comparative difference between questions considered *essential* to those that are *non-essential*.

Table 2.4. Purpose of Driving (Essential) Questions. http://grantwiggins.wordpress.com/2013/02/08/on-genuine-vs-bogus-inquiry-using-eqs-properly/

A good Essential Question:

(1) is *open-ended*, i.e., it typically will not have a single, final, and correct answer.
(2) is *thought-provoking* and *intellectually engaging*, meant to spark discussion and debate.
(3) calls for *higher-order thinking*, such as analysis, inference, evaluation, and prediction. It cannot be effectively answered by recall alone.
(4) points toward *important, transferable ideas* within (and sometimes across) disciplines.
(5) *raises additional questions* and sparks further inquiry.
(6) *requires support* and *justification*, not just an answer.
(7) *recurs* over time, i.e., the question can and should be re-visited again and again.
   (Wiggins, February 8, 2013, p. 1)

Table 2.5. The Difference Between a Driving Question and a Non-driving Question

Driving question	Non-driving question
How are body structures of an organisms related to how they interact and survive?	How many body parts does an insect have?
What is the relationship between popularity and greatness in literature?	What is the main idea in the novel, *The Great Gatsby*?
To what extent are science and common sense related?	What are the stages of the scientific process?

Two Types of Driving Questions

Wiggins and McTighe (2005) identify two main types of driving questions. These are *overarching* and *topical*. The main difference between the two is that *Overarching* is general and incorporates the big idea of a topic of study and therefore is best used at the beginning of a unit. The *Topical* driving question generally pertains to the particular topic of study within and individual lesson. If crafted in this manner, a unit of study will have one *overarching driving question* with each lesson plan incorporating a *topical driving question*. Table 2.6 outlines the general goal and provides examples of these differences.

Table 2.6. Overarching Versus Topical Driving Questions

Overarching questions Ideal for *Driving* the Unit	Topical questions Ideal for *Driving* the Lesson
• Focus on the big idea of a unit. • Similar to a unit goal but written as broad, open-ended question. • Typically, there is one for the entire unit of study.	• Will "drive" a particular lesson. • May be linked to a lesson's objectives. • Responding to topical questions can be a form of formative assessment for that lesson.
To Consider • Is it broad? • Can it be used across an expanse of time (month, semester, year)? • Will it generate multiple responses on what students have learned about the "big idea?"	**To Consider** • Is it open-ended to promote multiple student responses yet focused enough to link to the day's lesson? • Can all topical questions be used to respond to overarching question?
Examples • How can we save the Bay? • What is the relationship between structure/function and the survival of an organism?	**Examples** • How can we reduce the amount of schoolyard runoff? • How does structure and behavior of bees allow it to gather food from plants?

Crafting Driving Questions

Crafting driving question is very much aligned with the concept of *process writing* (Blake, 2020), where writing is recursive, collaborative, social, and critical. Such writing is trial-and-error, a constant movement from writing, revising and writing again. It is no simple task but one that takes time and effort. As Wiggins (2015) comments:

> Common first-draft questions typically are convergent low-level questions designed to support content acquisition. They either point toward the one official "right" answer, or they elicit mere lists and thus no further inquiry. (abstract). . . . Getting the questions right takes discipline, skill, and artfulness. But it's well worth the effort to ensure that students tackle inquiries that are important, intriguing, and revealing. (para 42)

Here are a few tips for crafting/writing driving questions.

(1) Be thoughtful and link specifically to what you want the students to *know* and *do*.

(2) Use one *Overarching* question with each *topical* question being part of the whole.
(3) Make sure the questions link to the lesson objective and the actual instruction.
(4) Always frame questions in "kid language."
(5) Post around the room to allow for continuous thought and reflection and allow for time to respond to these and potential new questions.
(6) Promote student-generated questions to promote student involvement. One way is to leave space on poster paper for students to write new questions.

Driving questions are fundamental in curriculum design. They set the stage for the unit and need to be well thought out for the learning process to be most effective. Successful teachers refer to the driving question throughout the lesson as it focuses the concepts and elicits critical thinking skills from the students. Driving questions are an important component of curriculum design and have the power to get students motivated for the learning.

A Note About Process Skills

As we can see the importance of determining a well-structured driving question, we must also consider how the content and process skills are an integral part of the whole reconstruction.

Using Bloom's taxonomy allows us to find action words that correspond to what we want students to *know* and *do*. Knowing content is usually easy, since much of how we teach and assess has traditionally been focused on content knowledge. *Process skills*, however, may be more difficult to discern yet focusing on content knowledge *and* process skills greatly expands the level of sophistication of your lessons and thus enhances student learning. When we move beyond simply teaching the content and integrate the process skills into learning, our assessments can too, move beyond the simple testing of knowledge. Here we lean on Padilla (1990) and his description of process skills (both Basic and Integrated Skills) (see Table 2.7). In reviewing this list, you may also notice that many of the process skills appear as action words in Bloom's Taxonomy, and a number of these skills are actually *higher-order thinking skills*.

Table 2.7. Process Skills as Listed by Padilla (1990). See *Research Matters* #9004. https://narst.org/research-matters/science-process-skills)

Basic Process Skills (Padilla, 1990)
Observing—gathering information about an object or event.
Measuring—measuring or estimating dimensions of an object or event. Can be in standard or non-standard units.
Inferring—using previous information/observations to make an *educated guess*.
Communicating—oral or verbal means (including sign language) and using words or graphic symbols to describe/explain.
Classifying—categorizing/grouping objects or events into categories based on pre-determined properties.
Predicting—using a pattern of data/observations/evidence to state a potential outcome.

A Note on Scope and Sequencing (S & S)

Scope and sequencing involves the breadth and order of what you will teach, with *scope=breadth/depth* and *sequencing=order*. Many times, S & S simply refers to the order of your sub-topics; what you plan to teach first, second, third, etc. Scope and Sequencing can also mean HOW you order your objectives within each sub-topic. Ordering your objectives is another level in your professional thinking; one where you clearly articulate the sequence of the content/process skills within your lessons and your unit. For example, if you believe that lower-order objectives must first be learned before applying higher-order thinking skills, then ordering objectives beginning with *define, memorize, repeat, record, list, recall,* and/or *name* will come before you ask students to *compare/contrast, analyze pros and cons, and explain the value of* a certain issue over another.

However, you could believe that students can and should *judge, assess, decide, measure, appraise, estimate, or evaluate* issues or ideas of a topic BEFORE they learn the specific definitions. If that is the case, then your higher-order thinking skills may come first in your teaching. Since lessons are constructed from objectives you will begin to notice that your beliefs in teaching, how you want to engage students in learning will determine the sequence of your objectives and thus, the sequence of your lessons within a particular topic. Constructing lesson plans and then organizing these into a unit is the topic of Step 3.

Putting it all Together: A Sample of a Full Scope and Sequence

Table 2.8 showcases a complete pre-service teacher's scope and sequence from the previously discussed Chesapeake Bay unit. Notice that this S & S has four components:

1. Unit Heading.
2. Topic for *Each* Day.
3. One objective for day (minimum).
4. Brief description of what you plan to do and what they will "know/do" by end.

Table 2.8. A complete Scope and Sequence from the Chesapeake Bay Deconstruction and Reconstruction.

Scope and Sequence
3rd Grade Science:

Big Concept: Chesapeake Bay

Lesson #1: Ice Breaker
Objectives:

1. The students will develop teacher/student relationships by creating a sailboat name tag and a "Chesapeake Bay name."

(Teacher Information: This name will be derived from a word related to the Chesapeake Bay and the student's name. The preferable name will consist of alliteration, but it may not be possible for all students to think of such a name, so any Bay-related name is acceptable.)

Activity: Students will create "Chesapeake Bay Name Tags" as well as create their science folders.

Lesson #2: Watersheds
Objectives:

1. The students will be able to define what a watershed is and how it relates to the Chesapeake Bay by constructing a watershed model.
2. The students will be able to predict how the water will flow by constructing a working model of a watershed.
3. Students will be able to identify which rivers and streams are a part of the Chesapeake Bay watershed by coloring and coding the rivers and streams.

STEP 2: THE RECONSTRUCTION   45

Table 2.8. Continued

Activity: The students will create a model of a watershed. They will also color rivers and streams that flow into the Bay on a copy of a map of the Chesapeake Bay watershed.

Lesson 3#: Pollution
Objectives:

1. The students will be able to explain how pollution impacts the Chesapeake Bay by creating a pollution experiment.
2. The students will be able to observe how point and non-point pollutants can alter the composition of Bay by creating pollution graphs.
3. The students will be able to investigate ways in which we can clean up pollution in the Bay by simulating a clean-up.
4. The students will be able to define and compare the different stages of the water cycle by creating a water cycle wheel.

Activity: Students will rotate through four different stations in order learn more about pollution and the water cycle. Station 1: students will be able to "create" and "clean=up" pollution. Station 2: the students will observe how pollution travels by spraying water on bread that has drops of food coloring on it. Station 3: students will make "pollution" graphs to see how pollution differs depending on which area of the bay that you are in. Station 4: students will learn about the water cycle by creating a "water cycle wheel."

Lesson #4: Mapping
Objectives:

1. The students will be able to identify and label the main features of a map by creating their own school maps.
2. The students will be able to identify and list natural and manmade items on the school ground by creating a school map.

Activity: Students will complete two worksheets on maps. They will then be able to go outside to create their own schoolyard maps.

Lesson #5: Physical Geography
Objectives:

1. The students will be able to observe the composition of different plants and/or living organisms in its environment by doing an experiment with hand lenses.
2. The students will be able to observe and record major factors that influence the "health" of their schoolyard by completing a schoolyard report card.
3. The students will be able to explain/describe how the Schoolyard Report Card related to what they observed at the stream by making a class presentation.

Activity: Students will grade their school by completing a schoolyard report card. They will then go down to the stream to observe and record different features of the stream, such as the temperature, different organisms they may see, clarity, etc.

Continued

Table 2.8. Continued

Lesson #6: Food Chain
Objectives:

1. The students will be able to label the Chesapeake Bay food chain by making a model.
2. The students will be able to define different animals/plants (that live in the Bay) by classifying them as producers, decomposers, or consumers.
3. The students will be able to recognize cause-and-effect relationships in the food chain by building a food chain pyramid.

Activity: The students will first complete a summative assessment of the information that we have covered so far this semester. Students will then build a food chain pyramid and explore what happens when the food chain becomes unbalanced. They will also create their own diagram of a food chain being sure to include decomposers, consumers, and producers.

Lesson #7: Habitats
Objectives:

1. The students will be able to identify the seven different habitats located in the Chesapeake Bay watershed by making a Chesapeake Bay diorama.

Activity: The students will learn about the different habitats that belong to the Chesapeake Bay watershed. They will also make shoebox dioramas of a Chesapeake Bay habitat using various materials (grass, paper, rocks, sticks, etc.).

Lesson 8:
Objectives:

1. The students will be able to demonstrate the relationship between producers and consumers by playing "Oh DEER!" (Taken from Project Wet).

Activity: The students will participate in the game "Oh Deer" to learn about the relationship between producers and consumers. The students will also partake in a "relay review" in order to review the major concepts that we focused on this semester.

What you want the students to know/do, you have written *objectives* and you have a tentative *scope and sequence* of your overall unit. Next you want to focus on the *how* of teaching, continuously thinking how you will engage students in the learning process. In Chapter 3, we showcase two instructional models we feel are well-situated for active learning.

Chapter 2: Reconstruction Activities

Activity One

- Rewrite the objectives so that each includes an AW and a BC.

    o They will create a model by showing the parts of the rainforest.
    o They will analyze the book by comparing the characters.
    o They will learn about kindness and watch a video.

Activity Two

- From the topic you have deconstructed from Chapter 1, use Bloom's taxonomy and construct four objectives that show what students will be able to know/do at the end of a lesson.

    Students will be able to . . .

    1. _____
    2. _____
    3. _____
    4. _____

    o Try to use both lower- and higher-order actions.

- Now complete at least two objectives that incorporate process skills.

    Students will be able to . . .

    1. _____
    2. _____

Activity Three

- Using these prompts create a well-designed objective. The first one is done for you.

1st graders learning about addition.
The students will be able to create number sentences by manipulating the pictures numbers and signs.

- o 1st graders learning about addition.
- o 2nd graders learning about the parts of a plant.
- o 5th graders learning about parts of the human body.
- o 7th graders learning about WWII.
- o 12 graders learning about the government.

Activity Four

- Look at each suggested teaching content area. For each, create two open-ended questions that could become the driving questions in a unit of study.

- o 2nd grade solar system unit
- o 4th grade fraction unit
- o 1st grade kindness unit
- o 5th grade persuasive writing unit
- o 2nd grade fairy tale unit

STEP 2: THE RECONSTRUCTION

Activity Five

Complete the Reconstruction model below using your own ideas for a unit of study.

Step #1. State the *Big Idea*

The Big Idea is . . .

_____

Step #2. Sequence *Sub-concepts* to create a *Scope and Sequence*

Scope and Sequence

| Topic #1 | Topic #2 | Topic #3 | Topic #4 |

Step #3. Use Bloom's Taxonomy and your "know and do" list and construct *Objectives* for each *Sub-concept*.

Objectives in Each Topic

Students will be able to . . .	Students will be able to . . .	Students will be able to . . .	Students will be able to . . .
1.	1.	1.	1.
2.	2.	2.	2.
3.	3.	3.	3.
Etc.	Etc.	Etc.	Etc.

Note

1 See the references for significant resources on Driving/Essential questions.

References

Anderson, L. W., & Krathwohl, D. R. (2001). *A taxonomy for learning, teaching and assessing: A revision of Bloom's taxonomy of educational objectives: Complete edition.* Longman.

Blake, B. E. (2020). *Critical process writing.* DIO Press.

Bloom, B. S. (1956). *Taxonomy of educational objectives, Handbook: The cognitive domain.* David McKay.

Bloom, B. S. (1984). *The search for methods of group instruction as effective as one-on-one tutoring.* Educational Leadership.

Hart, D. (1994). *Authentic assessment handbook: A handbook for educators.* Addison-Wesley.

Oakes, J. (1985). *Keeping track: How schools structure inequality.* Yale University Press.

Oakes, J. (2005). *Keeping track: How schools structure inequality* (2nd ed.). Yale University Press.

Padilla, M. J. (1990). *The science process skills. Research matters—To the science teacher* (No. 9004). National Association for Research in Science Teaching (NARST). https://narst.org/research-matters/science-process-skills

Sizer, T. R. (1984). *Horace's compromise: The dilemma of the American high school.* Houghton Mifflin.

Wiggins, G. (February, 8, 2013). On Genuine vs. Bogus Inquiry – Using EQs Properly. Authentic Education. https://authenticeducation.org/

Wiggns, G. (September 1, 2015). How to Make Your Questions Essential. Vol. 73(1). Alexandria, VA: Association for Supervision and Curriculum Development.

Wiggins, G., & McTighe, J. (1998). *Understanding by design.* Association for Supervision and Curriculum Development.

Wiggins, G., & McTighe, J. (2005). *Understanding by design* (expanded 2nd ed.). ASCD.

· 3 ·

STEP 3: PLANNING

Driving Question

Why am I teaching IT this way?

In this chapter, when we think of *planning*, we are referring to structuring a lesson plan to utilize in the classroom. While steps one and two *are* part of the larger planning process, where a lot of our work is accomplished, Step 3 is where we organize and structure what we have created into meaningful learning experiences for the students. Meaning: lesson plans.

In review, we begin with our five fundamental questions:[1]

The Content and Process Skills embedded in the topic.

(1) What do I want the students to know?
(2) What do I want our students to do?

The Instructional Model used for Teaching.

(3) Why am I teaching this?
(4) Why am I teaching IT this way?

Assessing Student Learning.

(5) *How will I know they have learned it?*

In steps one and two, we determined the *Big Idea*, or the central topic of the unit. We listed our *know* and *do* statements and we then re-word these statements into *objectives* using *action words* (AW) from Bloom's taxonomy. We also added one open-ended *driving question* (DQ) where both the objectives and the DQ could later be used as a lesson's formative assessment (see assessment in Chapter 4). Now we need to decide *how* we plan to teach and must choose the instructional model best suited for the lessons within the unit. This chapter will examine what we consider to be the essential components of a lesson, selecting an instructional model, and then ensuring that the lesson is interactive and engaging.

It is important for teachers to realize that there is a myriad of lesson plan formats available. Just looking on the internet, we can find a wide variety of templates, many of which are referred to as THE way to write a lesson plan. What is essential for teachers; however, is to be able to discern what parts are fundamentally important to include in *all* lessons. With this knowledge and understanding, you will be well-equipped to go to any district, in any state and create and implement well-designed lessons.

Fundamental Parts of a Lesson Plan

We first want to articulate what we consider to be key parts of a lesson, which includes responding to our two *why* questions (*Why am I teaching this? Why am I teaching it this way?*).

At the very least, a lesson plan should include:

(1) A *Purpose*—A clearly defined *purpose* that provides focus to the learning and should help keep the lesson cohesive. This answers: *Why am I teaching this?*

(2) A *Driving Question*—A single opened ended *driving question*, much like the purpose, helps to direct the learning.

(3) An *Objective*—No more than two *objectives*, each with an action word, formulated in the reconstruction phase which must correspond with the learning covered in the lesson. Objectives need to be accessible to students' understandings, formulated in a way to include all students in

the learning community, and used throughout the lesson to keep the students focused on the learning.

(4) *A Step-by-Step Written Process/Plan*—The *written process* or simply the lesson plan should, essentially, include what both students and teacher will do in the lesson. This answers: *Why am I teaching it this way* and will be dependent on the instructional model chosen.

At this point, number four is particularly important for teachers in training as they need to spend time thinking about strategic and engaging ways to create the lesson. There are two other important components that every lesson must include. The first is what we call *chunking*, where the learning experience is divided into varying learning settings. You always want to think of the different settings your students will be in during the lesson and then vary these throughout the learning. Examples of typical classroom learning settings and suggested abbreviations are:

(1) Whole Group (WG)
(2) Seatwork (STWK)
(3) Small Group (SG)
(4) Pairs (PRS)

The second major part of structuring focuses on *how long* or your *time frame* for each *chunk*. Managerial efficiency, or time management, is considered a key characteristic of exemplary teachers (Tobin and Fraser, 1988, 1990; also see Zemelman et al., 1993, 2012) and timing not only holds students accountable for their learning but also puts responsibility on the teacher to ensure that the learning is well-structured and paced. Facilitating chunking with effective timing during a lesson creates high-quality learning experiences which often take practice for teachers. A simplified sample is in Table 3.1.

Table 3.1. Sample *Chunking* with Timing Within a Lesson

Part I: Brainstorm in pairs (PRS) (5 Minutes)
Part II: Collection of Student Ideas. (WG) (10 minutes)
    (Teacher writes on board, creating a visual aid, such as an anchor chart)
Part III: Two pairs combine (4 in a group) to construct (2 PRS) (... 20 minutes)
Part IV: Wrap up. One student from each group reports findings. (WG) (10 min)

Interactive/Engaging Learning

While structuring helps lessons be more engaging, meaningful learning also must include opportunities for active involvement by the students. Too many times in classrooms, even after teachers have effectively deconstructed, reconstructed, and selected an instructional model, the facilitation of instruction is flat. Sometimes we see teachers missing a vital part of curriculum planning; making the learning come alive. In promoting this strategy, we embrace another one of Sizer's (1984) ten common principles, *Student as Worker, Teacher as Coach*, which necessitates that the students be actively engaged (physically and cognitively) in learning. Our goal is to promote more active learning, as opposed to passive learning. We have found that greater involvement in the learning helps students stay more connected and provides fewer occasions for off-task behaviors and classroom management issues.

We recommend reviewing a lesson after it is constructed, to be sure that there are many opportunities for direct student involvement and responsibility in the lesson. It is helpful to envision the children participating throughout the lesson, to fully see the potential engagement; essentially answering, *what will students be able to DO?*

Lessons, therefore, must include strategies that motivate, engage and challenge students within the learning process and again (we know, repetition) relates directly back to our last critical question; *Why am I teaching it this way?* Table 3.2 lists a variety of strategies to include in lessons to make them more interactive and engaging. They are listed by content area but clearly there is overlap and ways to incorporate most strategies across content areas.

Table 3.2. Interactive Strategies for Lessons

Language arts/social studies	Math/science
Read-alouds	Math stories
Picture walks	Quick writes
Venn diagrams	Brainstorming
K-W-L chart	Working with manipulatives
Story maps	Puzzles
Mind mapping	Number rhymes
Story starters	Concept maps
Interviews	Which belongs game
Creating news articles	Number associations
Creating a social media page	Graphic organizers
Debates	Math meetings

STEP 3: PLANNING

Choosing an Instructional Model

As we look at the components of lesson planning, we reminisce on the pre-service teaching days and the often-mandated exhaustive lesson plan forms we were given. In completing these we, as novice teachers, had to consider just about every scenario we might face in teaching a lesson. We had to write a purpose, list/explain pre-existing knowledge, list associated standards (Content-based—Like Next Generation Science Standards-NGSS, 2013 or Common Core State Standards-CCSS, 2010), write objectives, create a detailed, step-by-step procedure/sequence using the *correct* instructional model, list/articulate any accommodations for students in need, determine multicultural considerations/equity measures, articulate how to address multiple learning styles, formulate assessments and then "reflect" on said lesson.

As mentioned earlier, we do not think that these categories are unimportant. We do think; however, that these plans are often too detailed, daunting, and are essentially required without any real connection to the individual components needed to make a lesson truly effective. Simply put, we consider them too exhaustive, and quite frankly, inaccessible and unnecessary for pre-service, or even in-service teachers, to complete daily. While we certainly believe the need to know how to write lesson plans, we argue that a shorter, more abbreviated version, is better suited, particularly for student and novice teachers; ones where the *keep-it-simple* concept is important.

Choosing an instructional model clearly depends upon the goals and content of the lesson. First, the *Gradual Release of Responsibility (GRR)* (Pearson and Gallagher, 1983) is one often used in the teaching of English Language Arts (ELA) or Integrated Language Arts (ILA), and Social Studies. Second, we showcase the *Constructivist Learning Model (CLM)*, which has a long history in science and mathematics education. To reiterate, the key to choosing *any* model should focus on the teacher's intent of *engaging* students within the learning process.

The Gradual Release of Responsibility (GRR) Instructional Model

We have found that in English Language Arts (ELA), using the GRR (Pearson & Gallagher, 1983), or a modified version, is most effective, as it allows the student to take ownership of learning in a very concrete systematic manner. It is important for teachers, particularly those in training, to take time to learn how to effectively integrate the model as it can be used cross-curricular throughout all grade levels. First published in 1983, this instructional model's core structure remains the same, where the cognitive work within learning shifts slowly and deliberately, from the teacher, through modeling, to joint responsibility between teachers and students, and ultimately to the students, through independent practice and application of learning. The actual lesson plan is often distilled to three statements: *I Do*, *We Do*, and *You Do* which directly links to our approach which includes Dynamic Introduction, Structured Instruction, Chunking/Group Work and Independent Practice. Table 3.3 shows a detailed template of our modified GRR, where we provide suggestions for the purpose of each component.

Table 3.3. Gradual Release Model with General Descriptors of the Instructional Sequence

Candidate		Date/Time	
Subject/Skill		Grade Level	
Standard			
Central Focus/Driving Question			
Lesson Objective			
Materials/Instructional Decisions			
	Instructional Sequence A Step-by-Step Process		
(1) Dynamic introduction	Time Frame	Instructional Procedure	
		• Motivation and engagement of the students. • Short; ten to fifteen minutes, but well-developed introductions are necessary. • Links directly to overall purpose.	
(2) Structured Instruction		• To scaffold the information to meet the needs of all the learners and supported practice with the material. • Teacher modeling to increase the understanding of the skills. • Questioning and prompts might be included to help students gain a deep understanding of the learning. • Ideally creative classroom strategies which keep students engaged in the learning.	

Continued

Table 3.3. Continued

(3) Chunking/Group work (Include how you will work with different groups here-ELL, Gifted, IEP Learners)		• Small Group Instruction, often involving teacher and students, to better solidify their understanding. Could involve just students without teacher too. This part involves small groups of 2 or more students. • Allows a teacher to differentiate the instruction to meet the needs of all learners. • Teacher works with the students in small groups to scaffold the information for learners who are struggling or just need some additional time to grasp the material. • Enrichment in small groups for students who should be challenged with new learning opportunities.
(4) Independent Practice		• Students apply the skills taught in the lesson independently. • May be the formative assessment but we caution our students that there should be considerable practice prior to assessing.
Planned Closure (include homework here)		• Engage students in discussion of the lesson. • Provides opportunity for students to articulate what they learned. • Restate/reply to objective, driving question, or both.
Assessment		• A means to *show* learning

Dynamic Introduction, Structured Instruction, Chunking/Group Work, and *Independent Practice* are the four major parts of our Gradual Release Model (GRR). The details above outline what and how each should be incorporated into the lesson for effective instruction. This structure provides the support students need to gain independence in the learning process ultimately leading for opportunities to demonstrate understandings. Figure 3.1 showcases a sample of a literacy unit for third graders in which our modified GRR instructional plan is utilized.

Candidate   Date/Time

STAR Student

Subject/Skill   **Grade Level**
Literacy/Central Message   3rd Grade

Standard (s)
CCSS.ELA-Literacy.RL.3.1—Ask and answer questions to demonstrate understanding of a text, referring explicitly to the text as the basis for the answers.
CCSS.ELA-Literacy.RL.3.2—Recount stories, including fables, folktales, and myths from diverse cultures; determine the central message, lesson, or moral and explain how it is conveyed through key details in the text.
Central Focus
Identify the central message of a fictional story using key details from the text.

Lesson Objective
Students will be able to define central message by reading texts and finding key events in the stories.
Materials/Instructional Decisions
Computer and Projector

Internet for Videos

- https://www.youtube.com/watch?v=mUj_8VyY75w
- https://www.passiton.com/inspirational-stories-tv-spots/170-humble-and-kind

Central Message Anchor Chart
Central Message Popcorn Bag Graphic Organizer (Poster Size)
Popcorn kernel paper cutouts for poster
Central Message Popcorn Bag Graphic Organizer
Copies of "The Boy Who Cried Wolf"
Pencils

Continued

Paragraphs for independent work
Agree/Disagree cards.
Copies of books based on table groups reading levels.
Sets of three pictures for assessment

Learning Segment

Dynamic Introduction—10 minutes

1. I will begin the lesson by sharing two brief video advertisements with the students. Before I begin the videos, I'll set a purpose for watching. Students should be ready to share a few things they noticed in both videos. https://www.youtube.com/watch?v=mUj_8VyY75w

https://www.passiton.com/inspirational-stories-tv-spots/170-humble-and-kind

2. *What was the main information you learned from the videos?* Turn and talk to discuss.

Structured Instruction—40 minutes

1. After talking with a friend, I will ask students what they noticed in each video. Once thoughts have been shared among the group, I will have students "turn and talk" about why someone would create these advertisements. Students should discuss what the creator may want them to learn or take away from these advertisements. (Students should be able to explain that the purpose of these videos is to spread kindness or to encourage people to be kind to others every day)
2. Upon identifying the purpose as a group, I will introduce the term central message. *Has anyone ever heard of the term, central message? Why do you think a central message may be important? What is the central message of the videos?* I will review the objective with the students.
3. In groups, they will have chart paper to write everything they think is a central message. We will come together and share charts and circle the things which are similar on the charts as a whole group. We will then determine that the central message is what the author wants readers to learn from the story. I will describe; a central message is the lesson the author is trying to teach, something the author wants readers to take away from the story. I will also explain to students that the central message is often implied, meaning it is not directly stated in the story of most books. I will explain to students that we need to look at the key or main events of a story to help us identify the central message. I will also provide students with examples of central messages found within books they may have previously read.
4. I will informally check in with students. Students would put their thumbs up if they made sense of central message and are ready to move on with an example. If students are still confused, they will put their thumb down as a way of letting me know they need further explanation and aren't quite ready to move on.
I will give students the opportunity to ask questions, but I will also have a peer explain it to students in their own words.

STEP 3: PLANNING

5. Once all students are ready to move forward, I will introduce our central message popcorn graphic organizer. The bag portion of the organizer is our central message, and the popcorn kernel are our key details. We will add kernels (key details) to our bag to help us identify the central message.
6. Students put their thumbs up if they understand how to use the graphic organizer. I will inform students that I'm going to model how I would find the central message and key details of a story.
7. I will read "The Boy Who Cried Wolf" aloud, as students follow along in their copy of the book. As we are reading, students should be thinking about key events/details that are taking place in the story. I will give them post-it-notes to mark where they hear the key details in the story.
8. Students will turn and talk about what they think the key details are in the story.
9. I will begin modeling the skill and think aloud to demonstrate the connections made between the central message and the key details. I will make sure to support the message and details with the text from the book.
10. I will pick up one paper popcorn kernel and share a detail from our story but may not be very important when identifying the central message. I will say, *I remember that the story takes place near a dark forest just outside the village.* I would then ask students if they thought that detail would be helpful in figuring out the lesson of our story. Students should recognize that the setting is an important detail in general but more than likely it isn't going to help me figure out the lesson or the central message. I will have students put their thumbs up if they understand the example and why it isn't helpful to figure out the central message of the story.
11. I will continue thinking out loud and share a detail that would be helpful. *I think the boy yelling that there was a wolf twice when he didn't see a wolf at all, is an important detail from our story.* I will write the detail on the paper popcorn kernel and students will use their agree signs if they agree that this is an important detail. Using tape, I will place the kernel (detail) "inside" of our popcorn bag.
12. I will continue thinking out loud, sharing another important key detail. "I think the boy laughing at the trick he played on the villagers is also an important key detail." I will ask students to hold up their agree cards if they agree with this detail. Again, I will write this detail on a paper kernel and place it "inside" our bag.
13. I will let students know that because we have a short story, fewer details may be needed to identify the central message. I will ask them to make a guess if three details would be enough to identify the central message. With that, I will ask a student to share out another key detail they thought of. Students may say some of the following:

  - "The boy thought of a plan to amuse himself."
  - "A wolf actually came but when he yelled "Wolf, wolf!" none of the villagers came to help him."

Continued

- "The villagers said the boy wasn't going to fool or trick them again."

14. I will check with students again to ensure they agree with the key detail that was shared. I will have them hold up their agree cards is they agree. If students agree, I will write it down and place it "inside" our popcorn bag. If there is a discrepancy, we will discuss it as a group and help guide our classmates to a stronger detail.

15. After three details have been added to our bag, I'll continue modeling my think-aloud and talking about how these details might help to identify the lesson. I will pause and ask them if they understand. Put your hands on your bellies if this makes sense to you. If not review it again for the students.

- What does the author really want me to learn from this?
- Do they want to remember not to call wolves? Does he want me to remember not to ask others for help?
- What's a good lesson I could learn?

16. Students should turn and talk to come up with central messages. We will share them with each other understanding that there are different interpretations of a central message, but it is important to support it with detail from the story. We will agree on a central message, and I'll write it down on the popcorn bag as our central message. I will have students refer to the posted objective as they get ready for group work. We will make sure that we are working toward meeting the objective.

Chunking (Group work)—30 minutes

1. The students will be split into groups. Different leveled books will be used based on the reading levels of each group. I will post the directions on the board. They are to read the story with a partner and mark where the key details are in the story. They should fill out their worksheet listing the details and then come up with the central message of the story.
2. I will pull my gifted and IEP groups and work on the assignment together using the appropriate leveled readers. I will scaffold the information for my IEP students. The gifted students will read independently and write a paragraph demonstrating the central message with supporting details to back it up.
3. I will then ask them to put their thumbs up if they understand today's learning and will take any questions.

Independent Work-25 minutes

1. Have the students work independently with a paragraph and come up with the central message. (differentiate the paragraphs based on their reading levels and skill set)

Planned Closure-5 minutes

1. Was our objective met? How do we know that?
2. Can someone tell me what you learned today?

> 3. Can someone add to that and tell us what else you learned about central messages?
> 4. I will summarize it after the students share their learnings.
>
> **Assessment-15 minutes**
> 1. Give the students three pictures about a story. Have them define the central message of the pictures. Collect the work to grade.

Figure 3.1. Sample. Gradual Release of Responsibility Instructional Lesson Plan

A Constructivist Learning Model (CLM)

The second approach we will focus on is the Constructivist Learning model. A constructivist approach to learning is rooted in the writing and work of Dewey (1938), Vygotsky (1962, 1989), and Piaget (1962). Karplus and Thier (1967) first introduced a three-part model, *Exploration, Invention, and Discovery*, as part of the Science Curriculum Improvement Study (SCIS) program and was later modified by Lawson (1988) to *Exploration, Concept (Term) Introduction, and Concept Application*. By the late 1980s and early 1990s, Biological Science Curriculum Studies (BSCS, 1989, 1992) introduced the 5-E model and in 1991, Robert Yager published an article titled *The Constructivist Learning Model* (Yager, 1991).[2]

Today, much of the science school curricula is rooted in the BSCS 5E model, but we often teach the three parts (*Exploration, Concept Introduction, and Concept Application*) as we find it more manageable for daily classroom practice. We emphasize the refrain of *Explore before Explain* as well as the Deweyan notion of *science-as-method* (Dewey, 1910).

Frequently synonymous with an *inquiry model*, a CLM differs from most other instructional models in that the lesson begins with students engaged in an activity that promotes *exploration* through actively doing something (physically or cognitively) that directly relates to the big idea of the lesson. Our experience has shown us that, in particular, pre-service interns have considerable difficulty designing learning which *explores* first. Frequently, they simply want to tell the students and/or lecture to them about the intended lesson purpose. Table 3.4 shows a modified template using a CLM instructional model and Table 3.5 exhibits what it might look like as a written lesson plan.

Table 3.4. A Modified Template of a Constructivist Learning Model Framework for Science

A Generalized Heading

1. A Statement of Purpose
2. A single Topical Driving Question
3. What do you want them to *Know (Content)* and *Do (Process Skills)*?
    a. What do you want the students to know/learn by the end?
        i. Create a list or simply describe the content.
    b. What do you want students to be able to "DO?" (Active learning. See Process Skills list)
        i. Create a list or simply describe the process skills.
4. Material and Safety Considerations
    a. Create a list of materials and
    b. Describe any safety issues.

Written Objective(s):

(1) *The students will* . . . (Use *Action Words* from Bloom's Taxonomy and think A, AW, BC, and D of objective writing. KEEP SIMPLE. Consider one or more of the process skills to include in your lesson)
    a. KEY—AW and BC!

Your Formative Assessment—*How will I know they have learned "IT?"*

Constructivist Learning Model (CLM)
(Three Part—Karplus and Thier, 1967).
A Step-by-Step Process

Part I: Exploration/Brainstorm (A means to assess prior knowledge)

a. the letters [a, b, c] refer to the sequence of the lesson and what students/you will be doing.
b. Etc.

Part II: Concept Introduction. (A means to help organize ideas and/or "funnel" ideas toward the concept/topic)

a.
b. Etc.

Part III: Concept Application (A means to apply ideas/concepts to a new activity. Also consider *practice*)

a.
b. Etc.

Part IV: Wrap up. (A means to assess learning. Can be part of Concept Application or any other means of formative assessment. Must be linked to objectives.)

STEP 3: PLANNING

Table 3.5. Sample CLM Lesson Plan on Survival of the Fittest Lesson

Unit: Survival of the Fittest

1. Purpose—*Why are we doing this?*
   To gather, create, interpret, and analyze data to determine limiting factors and the "carrying capacity" for a given population of organism.
2. Topical *Driving Question* –
   Why do you think not all of the bears survived?
3. What will students *know and do?*

Know?
Define limiting factor.
Identify the essential factors of a habitat.

Do?
Describe how limiting factors influence a population.
Analyze the data they collect.
Apply data to the average bear survival rate.

Safety Considerations -
Make sure students are following directions and using materials appropriately

4. Materials –
Limiting Factors worksheet
Paper bags
Small, lettered pieces of paper
   M, B, I, N, P
Calculators

5. Objective (Action word and By clause)
Students will be able to describe the effects of limiting factors on a bear population by analyzing data about a habitat's limiting factors.

Formative Assessment (use open-ended questions and/or objective):
Limiting Factors worksheet

6. Procedure (step by step)

Part 1: Exploration (25 minutes):
   a. Students will go outside and complete the Limiting Factors bear activity.
   b. Supply students with a paper bag that will be used to hold the paper pieces they have collected during the activity.
   c. Set up 2 lines of tape across from each other as a starting point.
   d. Scatter paper pieces (labeled M, B, N, I, P) on the ground.
   e. Explain that one student will be injured and only has one leg and the other will be "Mama Bear" with 2 cubs that will need to collect extra food.
   f. Explain that once a student has picked up one piece they MUST go back to the starting line before grabbing another.
   g. The game will be completed once all of the paper has been picked up.
   h. Students will then be instructed to come inside with their paper bags.

Continued

Table 3.5. Continued

Part 2: Concept introduction: (10 min)
a. Bring students inside and have them sit at their desks.
b. Explain meanings of numbers and letter on the cards they have collected.
c. Have students add up total pounds of food they gathered and write it on their worksheet.
d. Tells students that each bear needs 80 pounds of food to survive.
– How many bears survived?
– How many pounds did the mother bear collect?
– Did the mother and her cubs survive if each cub needs half of what an adult bear needs? (double the food)
– How many pounds did the injured bear collect?
– Did the injured survive?
Part 3: Concept application: (10 mins)
a. Ask students to record how many pounds is each of the 5 categories of food they gathered.
b. Have students calculate the percentage of their food in each of the 5 categories with teacher assistance.
c. Provide students with the background information about black bears so that they are able to compare their data with the data of real black bears.
d. Bring students together to divide the total of all of the classroom bears by 80 pounds to determine how many bears can survive in that habitat.
Part 4: Wrap Up (must be linked to objectives): (5 mins)
a. Have students put away materials and pack up their things for dismissal.

The original 5 E was intended to be used as a unit plan with each E being a separate lesson in the overall unit (see BSCS, Science for Life and Living, 1988 and Bybee, 2014). We believe that it is best suited in this format. Yet, today, in many school systems, the 5E is considered a lesson plan, where teachers incorporate each part, *engage, explore, explain, elaborate,* and *evaluate* into every lesson. Our experience has shown, however, that this is very cumbersome, particularly for novice teachers, and often makes the lesson plan inaccessible and unmanageable as a usable, working document. Since our overall goal in this book is to simplify the planning process, we prefer *exploration, concept introduction,* and *concept application*; the three-part Constructivist Learning Model, outlined by Karplus and Their (1967). Nonetheless, whether teachers use the 5E or the three-part model we believe that the fundamental purposes of the CLM are addressed. To help clarify this point, Figure 3.2 showcases the comparison of the two models and the intended purposes for each part.

The Learning Cycle (Karplus and Thier, 1967)	The 5 Es (BSCS, 1992)
Exploration	**Engage/Explore**
"Manipulate," "Hands-on," "Minds-On," Observe, Ask Questions, Jump in, Do, Brainstorm, Evaluate, Make Decisions, Construct Models, Discuss, Demonstration. *The primary purpose for the first stages is to engage the students in activities that stimulate and assess prior knowledge about the concept and allow them opportunities to articulate current thoughts. Typically, this can be set up with a minimal amount of instructions, possibly with "Essential" or "Driving" Questions. Time limit is short. You may also consider this the "Motivator."*	
Term/Concept Introduction	**Explain**
Direct teacher role: collect and share ideas as whole class, KWL, discuss student conceptions and compare with current conceptions, direct instruction, mini-lesson, demonstration, assemble multiple ideas/solutions/answers and look for plausibility, introduce terminology. *The primary purpose for these stages is to collect student ideas and responses and compare to the intended concept. This can either be done through socratically, direct instruction, or a combination of either. The key is "EXPERIENCE BEFORE EXPLANATION." This stage can be, and tends to be more traditional in format. The idea is to Affirm and Confirm student findings/ideas from the Engage/Explore.*	
Concept Application	**Elaborate/Evaluate**
"Do," link previous experiences to new activities, apply concepts, extend, expand, and reinforce the concept(s), use terms, generate questions, *The primary purpose for these stages is to apply the concept to new learning situations, to allow students more experiences to move knowledge/understanding from short to long-term memory, and to use as alternative assessments. In the Evaluate stage, you use the student results to not only assess their learning but also to assess your teaching.*	

Figure 3.2. A Comparision of the Three Part and the 5E Constructivist Learning Model (Also called the *Learning Cycle*).

A Brief Note on Assessment

As we have seen in this chapter, planning effective well-designed lessons is essential for teachers. The structuring of a lesson and ultimately deciding how to teach the lesson is central to students' learning and ultimately their ability to achieve. The two approaches we have discussed, the constructivist and gradual release models, provide the best opportunities for students to be active and engaged in the learning. These systematic approaches are applicable across content areas. What remains consistent in our experiences is the key parts of any lesson form must answer these two questions: *Why am I teaching it?* and *Why am I teaching it this way?*

As we have completed the deconstruction, reconstruction, and planning phases of our curriculum design, we must examine if students have learned the material. This is covered in our last chapter as we explore assessments. As educators we must take the time to understand where students are in their learning so that we can positively impact students' understandings and ultimately their achievement.

Chapter 3: Planning Activities

Activity One

Think about the *Learning Structure* or *Chunking* in a Lesson. Explain how you will incorporate whole group, seatwork, small group, and pair instruction into one of your lesson plans. Be specific and make sure to think about how each different structure will help you to meet the needs of the learners in the specific group.

Activity Two

Compare a Gradual Release Model with the Constructivist Model. Explain how the two models are similar and how they are they different.

STEP 3: PLANNING

Activity Three

Look at the interactive strategies for a lesson (Table 3.2). Pick two and write how you could include the activities in a lesson about non-fiction reading for third graders. Look at another interactive strategy for a lesson. Pick two and write how you could include the activities in a lesson about nutrition for fourth graders.

Notes

1 To reiterate. If these questions cannot be answered with a sound educational rational, then, as professionals we must rethink what we are doing and return to early steps.
2 Biological Science Curriculum Studies (BSCS) has a thorough historical examination on the origins of the constructive learning model. See Bybee, et al. (2006). The BSCS 5E Instructional Model: Origins and Effectiveness. NIH. https://bscs.org/reports/the-bscs-5e-instructional-model-origins-and-effectiveness/

References

Biological Sciences Curriculum Study (1988). Science for life and living. Dubuque, IA: Kendall/Hunt

Biological Sciences Curriculum Study (BSCS). (1989). *New designs for elementary school science and health*. Kendall Hunt.

Biological Sciences Curriculum Study. (1992). *Science for life and living. Integrating science, technology, and health: Implementation guide*. Kendall/Hunt.Bybee, R., Taylor, J., Gardner, A., Scotter, P., Carlson, J., Westbrook, A., Landes, N. (2006). *The BSCS 5E instructional model: Origins, effectiveness, and applications*. BSCS.

Bybee, R. W. (2014). The BSCS 5E instructional model: Personal reflections and contemporary implications. *Science and Children, 51*(8), 10–13.

Dewey, J. (1910). Science as subject-matter and as method. *Science, 31*(787), 121–127.

Dewey, J. (1938). *Experience and education*. Macmillan.

Karplus, R., & Thier, H. D. (1967). *A new look at elementary school science*. Rand McNally. University Press.

Lawson, A. E. (1988). A better way to teach biology. *The American Biology Teacher, 50*(5), 266–278. https://doi.org/10.2307/4448733

National Governors Association Center for Best Practices & Council of Chief State School Officers. (2010). *Common core state standards*.

NGSS Lead States. (2013). *Next generation science standards: For states, By states*. The National Academies Press.

Pearson, D. P., & Gallagher, M. C. (1983). The instruction of reading comprehension. *Contemporary Educational Psychology*, 8(3), 317–344.

Piaget, J. (1962). The stages of the intellectual development of the child. *Bulletin of the Menninger Clinic*, 26, 120.

Sizer, T. R. (1984). *Horace's compromise: The dilemma of the American high school*. Houghton Mifflin.

Tobin, K., & Fraser, B. J. (1988). Investigations of exemplary practice in science and mathematics teaching in Western Australia. *Journal of Curriculum Studies*, 20(4), 369–371.

Tobin, K., & Fraser, B. J. (1990). What does it mean to be an exemplary science teacher? *Journal of Research in Science Teaching*, 27(1), 3–25.

Yager, R. E. (1991). The constructivist learning model: Toward real reform in science education. *The Science Teacher*, 58(6), 52–57.

Vygotsky, L. (1962). *Thought and language*. (E. Hanfmann & G. Vakar, Eds.). MIT Press.

Vygotsky, L. (1989). *Thought and language* (rev. ed., A. Kozulin, Ed.). The MIT Press.

Zemelman, S., Daniels, H., & Hyde, A. (1993). *Best practice: New standards for teaching and learning in America's schools*. Heinemann. See Zemelman, Daniels, and Hyde (2012) Best Practice, Fourth Edition: Bringing Standards to Life in America's Classrooms.

Zemelman, Daniels, and Hyde (2012) Best Practice, Fourth Edition: Bringing Standards to Life in America's Classrooms. Portsmouth, NH: Heinemann.

· 4 ·

ASSESSING STUDENT LEARNING

Driving Question

How will I know they have learned it?

Assessing students' learning is essential to good teaching. Everything else we have completed in our curriculum design prior to this step; the *deconstruction*, the *reconstruction* and the *planning* leads us to asking; *How will I know they have learned it?* Simply put, our students must show their learning. Through high-quality well-developed assessments, students can demonstrate their understandings, while also providing teachers with the essential data to move forward in their teaching. Quality assessments must focus on engagement and higher-order thinking. Oftentimes assessments are not active, as teachers find it easier to give a multiple-choice test, which is less demanding to facilitate and grade. However, presenting students with varied engaging opportunities to show their understanding, provides a better indicator of their learning. Assessments should not just have students restate content knowledge in isolation but offer opportunities to think critically and demonstrate deeper understandings of a topic. At the very beginning of this book, we asked the following fundamental questions where each one directly relates to the ultimate goal of student learning and how to showcase this learning.

- *What do I want the students to know?*
- *What do I want our students to do?*
- *How will I know they have learned it?*

As we work to create effective assessments, it is essential that these assessments mirror the students' learning (linked to instruction) and be an *authentic* measurement of learned material. Used here, the term, authentic assessment, embodies Hart's (1994) definition, "An assessment is authentic when it involves students in tasks which are worthwhile, significant, and meaningful" (p. 9), like the tasks they completed during the lessons. We also align our thinking with Sizer's (1984) concept of the "exhibition of mastery," where students are allowed to demonstrate/showcase learning in differing ways, ones that are beyond a paper/pencil test.. They push engagement and allow students to show what they have learned through a variety of means. The next sections will analyze alternative means of assessments which keep our students active learners, as they apply their knowledge.

Types of Assessments-Formative and Summative

In general, assessments can be broken down into two main types: formative and summative. Formative assessments refer to those measures conducted within a lesson or at the end of a lesson, as the learning is being *formed*. These assessments provide teachers with the knowledge of what students are understanding at different points during the lesson. There are a range of formative assessments that can be incorporated into lessons. These assessments help teachers determine the direction of the lesson. It provides a mechanism for teachers to pose the questions to themselves, *Do we need to review, go on, or even enrich?*

Unlike formative assessments, *summative* assessments, are a summation of learning and usually occur at the end of a unit to *sum-up or* evaluate what was learned. While distinguishing between formative and summative assessments is necessary, we must also recognize that there are many types of quick assessments or check-ins to assess students' understanding throughout a lesson.

Strong educators often incorporate formative and quick assessment checks throughout a lesson and include a summative assessment at the end of the lesson or the unit of study.

Multiple Means of Assessment

Assessments, like other parts of a lesson, must also provide multiple means for students to demonstrate or show what they know. Grounded in Gardner's early work (1983), incorporating a variety of teaching and assessment types is critical to the overall learning process and central to our curriculum method. For example, a student may excel in interpersonal skills while another student may be more artistically inclined (later we will see how this can be assessed using *multi-dimensional* rubrics). Variations of learning and assessing should then provide opportunities for students to showcase what they know in what Gardner (2011) would call, their natural intelligence, commenting:

> There must be more to intelligence than short answers to short questions-answers that predict academic success; and yet, in the absence of a better way of thinking about intelligence, and of better ways to assess an individual's capabilities, this scenario is destined to be repeated universally for the foreseeable future. (p. 4)

As we think back to our own educational experiences, and encourage teachers to do the same, we often remember those experiences that allowed for more engaging means of showing or exhibiting what we knew. We encourage the use of assessment approaches to show understanding throughout a lesson. Incorporating quick assessment checks/all student responses provide that immediate indication of where students are in learning and understanding. It helps to inform teachers of a need to either slow down or reteach a portion of the lesson. A good rule of thumb is to incorporate *quick assessment checks* and/or *all student responses*, at least three to five times during a lesson. For example, teachers can use thumbs up if you understand or yes/no cards to show agreement. The frequent checks also keep students both engaged and active in the learning. Following is a look at multiple means of assessment methods to get students to apply their learning in a more engaging manner (Table 4.1).

Table 4.1. Formative and Summative Multiple Means of Assessments

Formative	Summative	Quick assessment checks/ all student responses
Exit tickets	Design a poster	Hands on your head if you agree
Write one thing you learned and one thing you are surprised at in the learning	Create a brochure	Show me the number with your fingers
Write a paragraph to an alien outlining the concept we just talked about in our lesson	Create a word map	Yes/no cards up
Fill out the graphic organizer comparing today's work with yesterday's learning	Perform a skit	Green light/red light on
Create and solve your own math problem	Create your own test and provide the answer sheet	Go to one side of the room if you agree
Draw a picture of the concept we just learned about	Make a presentation to the class.	Stand up if you agree
Write a letter to the character in the book	Create a web page to inform others about the content	Thumbs up if you agree/ Thumbs down if you disagree
Create song lyrics to go with the story	Create a magazine cover about the content/Write an article for the magazine.	White boards to show quick answers.
Sequence the steps of the learning	Complete a test	Draw on dry erase boards to show a quick picture or a response.

These multiple means of assessments provide many opportunities for students to show what they have learned and each type offers valuable data for the teacher as they are making instructional decisions. As we select the different means of assessments, we continuously refer to our original first two questions.

(1) *What do I want the students to know?*
(2) *What do I want our students to do?*

Components of Well-Designed Assessments

Working with teachers, particularly those in training, it is evident how difficult it can be to find the time to design assessments. As teachers, we often use all our energy in creating hands-on activities in the prior parts of the lesson and simply forget, or "run out of time" to assess learning. To ease this part of curriculum design, we have found that following four simple steps makes the process easier (see Figure 4.1).

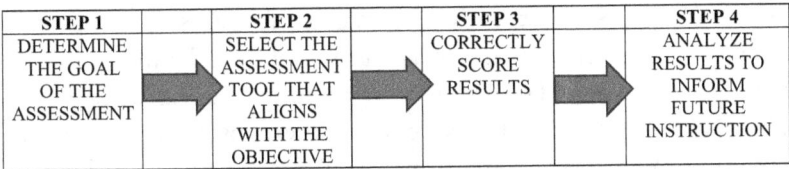

Figure 4.1. Assessment Sequence

Step 1 provides an essential starting point, as we create assessments. Understanding the *goal* of the assessment provides clarity on the entire process and as we repeatedly ask ourselves; *How will I know they have learned it?* And then ask; *How will they be able to show or demonstrate their learning?*

Step 2 ensures that the assessment is *aligned* with the objective. We must stop and ask if we are measuring what the objective is covering and are we assessing the same skills that were in the lesson? If not, then the alignment is off between the two and there needs to be a change made in the assessment, the intended objective, or in the teaching.

Step 3 requires us to determine *what type of scoring* tool to use. The ease and efficacy of scoring the assessment will depend on this tool and must adequately determine what reteaching is needed, or where there is mastery of the material. Students should understand how the assessment will be graded, prior to completing the task as this helps to provide focus for the assessment.

Step 4 involves *analyzing the results* to inform future instructional decisions. This helps us make the choices about what the lesson will look like tomorrow. Assessments should be graded in a timely fashion to provide the support students need. Thus, the assessment should also be regarded as a tool to improve future learning.

These four steps ensure that the assessment is meeting its intended goals and is positively impacting student learning. Ultimately, through a well-designed assessment, the data is used to improve educational outcomes for students.

Deciding on What to Assess

One of the more challenging aspects of teaching is to decide not only how students will show learning but what learning (Knowledge) they will show. As previously discussed (see Table 4.1), making decisions on formative versus summative is pertinent because decisions will need to be made on not only the types of assessments, but when to use them. In general, assessments such as: quizzes, exit tickets, activities, short answer responses, graphic organizers or even self-assessments, tend to be formative in nature and are used throughout lessons. Tests, projects, essays, portfolios, alternative and performance tasks, or any form that is used at the end of a unit are summative in nature.

One simple and systematic way to decide on assessment types beforehand is to brainstorm and collect ideas of how students show their understanding. Such forethought provides an assessment road map and aligns quite well with our process. We find it to be valuable because it allows us to identify if we are excessively assessing one area over the other (content versus process skills, OR lower lever skills over higher order ones).

Figure 4.2 is one example of an assessment collection chart and one adopted from Wiggins and McTighe (2005). We find this useful because it has the main unit components in one place (*Big Idea, Objectives, Driving Questions, etc.*) and allows us to consider varying means of assessment. Figure 4.3 then shows how this may look in a real unit.

While the four-step process and the collection of assessment evidence are necessary for a well-executed assessment, it is equally important to give students the tools for success. Ensuring that students know beforehand the expectation of an assessment is imperative to get a true indication of their learning. An effective way to achieve this is by incorporating rubrics into the assessment repertoire. In the next section, we share types and structures of rubrics and how teachers may go about crafting their own to meet the needs of students.

ASSESSING STUDENT LEARNING

Big Idea of Unit	
Driving Questions	
What do we want students to know?	What do we want students to do?
Why am I teaching it this?	Why am I teaching it this way?
Unit Objectives	
1. 2. 3. Etc.	

Collection of Assessment Evidence		
Type (Generally Used)	List Each time used and Formative or Summative (F or S)	What Assessed and Additional Notes
Quizzes (Formative)		
Activities (Formative)		
Tests (Summative)		
Work Samples (Formative and Summative)		
Presentations (Formative and Summative)		
Word Map (Specific to ELA?)		
Variety of Writing (Formative and Summative)		
• Respond to Driving Questions and/or Objectives. • Expository		
Performance Tasks (Usually Summative)		

Figure 4.2. Generating Assessment Ideas for a Unit (Adopted from Wiggins and McTighe, 2005)

Big Idea of Unit	
How do we create new words?	
Driving Questions	
What do we want students to know? Students should understand that by changing the beginning letters, new words can be created.	What do we want students to do? Students will use new letters to change the existing words into new words.

Continued

Why am I teaching it this?	Why am I teaching it this way?
It is an important skill to understand how words have connections to other words by often sharing the sounds and letters. This will help to build students' decoding and fluency skills.	By giving students a concrete opportunity to move letters, they will better understand how new words are formed and identify the connections between words. This concrete activity will help to solidify their understanding and their fluency with reading.

Unit Objectives

1. Students will change the beginning and ending sounds to create new words by playing a game.
2. Students will be able to create new words by using their own word bags.
3. Students will be able to formulate new words in a meaningful manner by writing a paragraph.

Collection of Assessment Evidence

Type	List Each time used and Formative or Summative (F or S)	What Assessed and Additional Notes
Quizzes	Lesson 4—S	Give students different words to create other words.
Activities	Lesson 1—F	Give each student a bag of words and cards with letters and have them create new words.
Tests		
Work samples		
Presentations		
Word Maps	Lesson 2—F	Give students word map and have them list all the words they could make with the core word.
Variety of Writing		
• Driving Question/ Objective Responses • Expository		
Performance Tasks	Lesson 3—F	Using the word bags generate a paragraph.

Figure 4.3. Sample of Unit Assessment Ideas for Unit: Creating New Words

Rubrics. What, Why, and Types

Simply stated, a rubric is the descriptive criteria for success in the assessment. Instead of simply a YES/NO response, rubrics provide an opportunity to apply higher-order thinking skills, where students are encouraged to explain and rationalize their learning. In providing a detailed description, often stated, *In my best work*, we allow students to know ahead of time what and how they need to show learning. This lets the student take ownership and initiative in demonstrating their knowledge.

Students should have the chance to review the rubric before starting an assignment. This provides another mechanism for them to be thorough on their work. The teacher's role is to make sure that students are clear on the expectations stated in the rubrics. As we work on creating well-designed assessments, our primary intent is to provide students a clear pathway for success in the assessment. A rubric should not just be used as a grading tool but also as a guide to ensuring student success.

There are different types of rubrics and selecting the one that is appropriate is important and determining the criteria and depth you want the students to master will help in the selection of the type of rubric. The most effective rubrics should have the following parts:

- Include all contents of the learning.
- Align with the goals of the objective.
- Delineate the differences in the levels with defined criteria.
- Allow for objective grading.
- Drive the project/assignment.
- Be given to students prior to the task.
- Be on a single sheet of paper for ease of viewing.
- Be given to students prior to the task.

Two General Types of Rubrics

Regardless of the rubric chosen all components of effective rubrics are essential to include. There are many different types of rubrics and selecting the one that is best for the assignment is important. The two general types of rubrics often used are the *Holistic and Multi-Dimensional*. *Holistic Rubrics* look at the "whole" of the student work, often describing specific details/criteria for a range of responses. Figure 4.4 shows a holistic rubric for ELA that assesses the entity of a written paragraph, where the writing is viewed as a whole. Figure 4.5 shows the holistic criteria for a write-up of a science inquiry project. In both, not only are the criteria for success provided but also the assessment components and written requirements.

Score	Criteria for Success
4	Organized writing with clear main idea.
	Details are well-developed and complete and support claims.
	Varied word choice.
	Grammatically accurate, including spelling and punctuation.
3	Mostly organized with main idea articulated.
	Includes many details to support claims.
	Uses mostly varied word choices.
	Some errors in grammar including spelling and punctuation.
2	Lacks organization.
	Only a few details are included.
	Lacks varied words.
	Many errors exist in grammar including spelling and punctuation.
1	Illogical flow of writing.
	Limited or no details included.
	Limited word choice.
	Mostly errors exist in grammar including spelling and punctuation.

Figure 4.4. Holistic Rubric for Expository Writing

GUIDELINES FOR SEVENTH GRADE LABORATORY
AND ACTIVITY WRITE-UPS

Listed below are the areas of assessment that I will look at when I read and grade each laboratory write-up. You will be graded on a scale of 1-5 with 5 being the best work you can do.

ASSESSMENT COMPONENTS

1. Science content.

2. Science process. Which includes:
   - Ability to identify the problem to be solved.
   - Ability to identify the variables involved with the problem.
   - Ability to make a plan to solve the problem, identify the manipulated and responding variables, and to control all other variables in the problem.
   - Ability to carry out the plan and collect data through the use of proper science/math tools and equipment.
   - Ability to organize and to represent data in table and graphic form.
   - Ability to interpret data and describe any patterns present.
   - Ability to make concluding statements based on what the data indicate and the original problem.
   - Ability to write a clear, neat, and organized write up.

WRITE-UP REQUIREMENTS

☞ *EACH WRITE-UP SHALL HAVE THE FOLLOWING PARTS* ☜

✓ A Proper Heading which includes the following.

Full Name   *Title Lab or Activity*   Date

✓ An Identified Purpose.
     example   "We were trying to find out . . . . ."

✓ A Description of the plan used to carry out the task.

✓ When necessary a neat and properly labeled data table and/or graph.

✓ Concluding statements that have sufficient detail.
     example   "We found out . . . . ."

✓ Responses to any questions asked.

Continued

✱ ASSESSMENT SCALE ✱

POINT VALUE	CATEGORY	DESCRIPTION
5	Excellent	• Shows complete understanding of the problem. Excellent Effort. • Write-up is complete with clearly defined purpose, plan, and concluding statements. All questions are answered in complete sentences. • Clearly labeled manipulated and responding variables. • Table and Graph are present, are clearly labeled, and have proper scaling, units, with line graphed accurately.
4	Very Good	• Shows complete or near complete understanding of problem. Excellent Effort. • Write-up is near complete with somewhat clearly defined purpose, plan, and/or coherent concluding statements. All questions are attempted but may not be answered in complete sentences. • Variables are apparent but may or may not be identified. • Table and Graph are present, but may be partially labeled. Line is plotted correctly.
3	Good	• Shows incomplete understanding of problem. Good Effort. • Write-up is incomplete, with missing heading. Purpose, plan, and/or concluding statements are unclear and/or missing. Questions are attempted, but are not answered in complete sentences. • Variables are apparent but may not be identified. • Table and Graph are present, but are unclear, partially, or improperly labeled. Line may or may not be plotted correctly.
2	Fair	• Shows incomplete understanding of problem. Lack of Effort evident. • Write-up is incomplete, and/or incoherent. Purpose and concluding statements are unclear or missing. Incoherent or missing plan. Questions are missing or are incomplete. • Variables may or may not be apparent, but are not identified. • Table and/or Graph are missing. If present they are confusing and improperly labeled. Line is plotted incorrectly.
1	Poor	• Shows no understanding of problem. Very little effort evident. • All parts of Write-up and Plan are incoherent and/or completely missing. • Variables are not apparent. • Table and Graph are missing or are incoherent with improper labeling and plotting.
0	No Effort	• No effort was made to complete the activity.

Figure 4.5. Seventh Grade Holistic Science Rubric

With *multi-dimensional* rubrics, the term "multi," refers to the fact that more than one category is assessed. The dimensions, or categories, are decided in advance with the criteria shared with students before they begin the assessment process. For example, in Mathematics problem-solving, teachers may be looking at how well students perform on the following dimensions/categories (Table 4.2) and in ELA the dimensions for writing a well-crafted paragraph may include those shown in Table 4.3. Examples of *multi-dimensional* rubrics are shown in Figures 4.6 (Mathematics) and 4.7 (ELA paragraph writing).

Table 4.2. Multi-Dimensional in Mathematical Problem-Solving

Dimension	Purpose
Content Knowledge	The ability to show correct mathematical knowledge, which may include number identification, correct calculations and/or correct use of mathematical tools.
Communication (Telling)	The ability to tell others, in a clear and succinct manner, how the problem was solved.
Problem-Solving	The ability to actually solve the problem and is linked to content knowledge.

Table 4.3. Multi-Dimensional Rubric for ELA Paragraph Writing

Dimension	Purpose
Organization	The ability to structure and order the writing in a logical sequence.
Supporting Evidence/Details	The ability to use evidence and details to support written statements.
Sentence Structure	The ability to present writing in academic language sentence structure.
Mechanics	The ability to use proper grammar and punctuation.

TIMS THIRD GRADE MULTIDIMENSIONAL RUBRICS

UNDERSTANDING MATHEMATICAL CONTENT

Level 4:
- Shows *complete* understanding of mathematical concepts embedded in problem; identifies properties and/or applications of the concept;
- Translates between different modes of representation;
- Uses tools and algorithms *correctly*;
- Computes math facts *correctly*, where applicable.

Level 3:
- Shows *nearly complete* understanding of the problem's mathematical concepts;
- *May make minor errors in translating* between representations or *in use of tools.*;
- Uses algorithms *correctly*;
- May contain *minor* computation errors.

Level 2:
- Shows *limited* understanding of the problem's mathematical concepts;
- *May contain major errors* in translating between representation or *in use of tools.*;
- Uses algorithms *incorrectly*;
- May contain *serious* computational *errors*.

Level 1:
- Shows *no* knowledge of the problem's mathematical concepts;
- *Does not translate* between representations;
- Uses algorithms *incorrectly if at all*;
- *Contains serious* computational *errors*.

SOLVING PROBLEMS

Level 4
- Interprets problem question correctly and identifies *all major* elements of the problem and the relationships between them;
- Reflects a *systematic, complete & efficient* strategy for solving problem;
- Makes *appropriate* use of tools (such as graphs, pictures, or tables) to organize relevant information;
- Looks back at problem and draws *appropriate* conclusions;
- May use relevant outside information.

Level 3:
- Interprets problem question correctly and i.d.'s *most of* the important elements of problem(s) *and the relationships between them;*
- Reflects *systematic, and complete or nearly complete* strategy;
- *May use tools (such as graphs, pictures, or tables) to organize information, possibly with minor errors;*
- *May look back at problem and draw conclusions.*

Level 2:
- Identifies *some* important elements of the problem(s), but shows *little understanding of the relationships between them.*;
- Gives *some evidence of* solution process, but strategy *may be incomplete or unsystematic*;
- May use tools *incorrectly & with little understanding* of their purpose.

Level 1:
- *Fails to identify the important* elements of the problem(s);
- Gives no relevant evidence of a solution process or *may use inappropriate strategy*;
- Any use tools totally incorrect & showing no understanding of their purpose.

COMMUNICATING

Level 4:
- Gives a *complete* response including a clear explanation &/or description;
- Presents *strong, sound* supporting arguments;
- Uses *pertinent* symbolic &/or visual representations *to support* explanations and *clearly explains their application*;
- *Clear and correct* use of terminology;
- Discusses *relevant* connections between this and other mathematical situations.

Level 3:
- Gives *fairly complete and clear* explanations or descriptions;
- Presents *logically sound* supporting argument(s), *possibly w/ minor gaps*;
- Use of symbolic and/or visual representations *may be incomplete, slightly incorrect*, or their application to the problem *may not be clearly explained;*
- *Inconsistent or unclear* use of terminology;
- May discuss connections between this and other mathematical situations.

Level 2:
- Explanation(s) and communication may be *ambiguous or unclear*.
- Argument(s) may be *incomplete*, or based on a *logically unsound* premise.
- Symbolic and/or visual representations may be used, but *no effort is made to tie* them *to the solution* of the problem.;
- *Totally incorrect or nonexistent* use of terminology.

Level 1:
- Explanations, if any, *totally unclear and irrelevant*;
- *No arguments* to support solution;
- Drawings, if any, *completely misrepresent* the problem and *no effort is made to tie* them *to the solution* of the problem; .
- *Totally incorrect or nonexistent* use of terminology.

Figure 4.6. TIMS Third Grade Multi-Dimensional Mathematics Rubric

	Criteria and Related Score			
Dimension	3	2	1	0
Organization	The paragraph is highly organized including a topic sentence and supporting evidence. The paragraph is fully developed.	The paragraph is organized including a topic sentence and evidence. The paragraph is developed.	The paragraph is not complete and lacks a well-developed topic sentence and supporting evidence. There is a lack of clarity in the development of the paragraph.	The paragraph is disorganized and with little attempt to show a topic sentence and supporting evidence.
Supporting Evidence/Details	There is well-developed, accurate supporting evidence. The support is logical.	There is some accurate evidence. The support is mostly logical.	The evidence is not clear or complete. The evidence is illogical.	The evidence is omitted.
Sentence Structure	All the sentences are well-written structurally and are complete.	Many of the sentences are well-written structurally.	The sentences lack structure and there are sentence fragments and run-ons.	The sentences have little structure with many sentence fragments and run-ons.
Mechanics	Students use correct spelling, capitalization, and punctuation throughout the paragraph.	Students mostly uses correct spelling, capitalization, and punctuation throughout the paragraph.	There are many errors with spelling, capitalization, and punctuation throughout the paragraph.	There are errors with spelling, capitalization, and punctuation in every sentence in the paragraph.

Figure 4.7. Rubric for a Well-Developed Paragraph with Supported Details

Student work using Multi-Dimensional Rubric

The following figures show the ideal result of student work with the multi-dimensional mathematics rubrics. This rubric come from the Teaching Integrated Mathematics and Science (TIMS) program based out of the University of Illinois at Chicago (UIC). Figure 4.8 shows student work from a multi-step problem called *The Carrot Project*. In the pre-rubric attempt the student does exactly what is asked. She diagrams the length of the carrot and

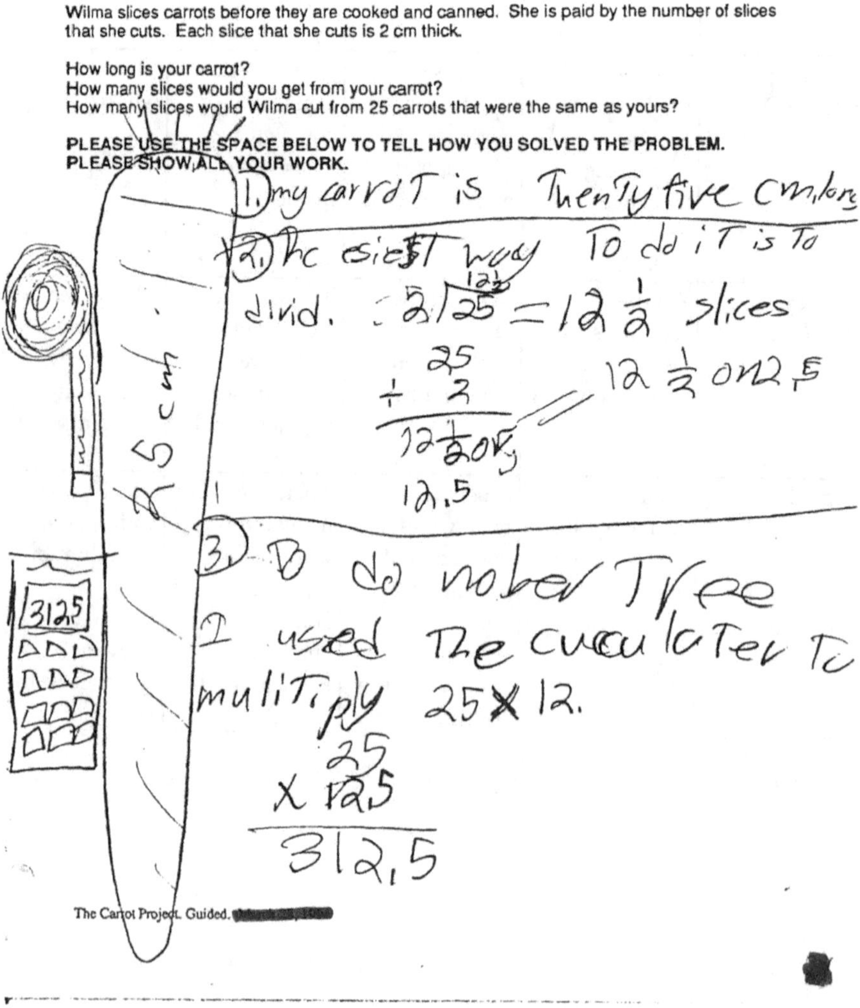

Figure 4.8. Carrot Project Student Work. Before Rubric Introduction

then shows how many slices she has and tells us how many slices she would cut if she had twenty-five carrots. While the solution is correct, the detail in the explanation is not.

In the post-rubric attempt, when the criteria for success were reviewed and discussed with the class and also posted around the room as *In My Best Work* posters (Table 4.4), students were given another multi-step *Carrot Project* problem. The student work in this example shows a marked difference in all dimensions, particularly in the written response (Figure 4.9).

Table 4.4. TIMS Multi-Dimensional Mathematics Rubric in "Kids" Language

Knowing	Solving	Telling
IN MY BEST WORK		
I show that I understand the math ideas.	I read the problem carefully and figure out what it is really asking. I list all the important pieces of the problem and think about how they fit together.	I list all of the steps that I used to solve the problem. I also tell what each number refers to (such as 15 boys or 6 inches).
I show the same math ideas in different ways (such as using both a graph and a table).	I come up with a good plan for solving the problem and I carry out the plan.	I explain why I solve the problem the way I did so people can see why my method makes sense.
I show I can use math tools and rules correctly.	I use tools like graphs, pictures, tables, or number sentences to help me solve the problem.	If I used tools like pictures, tables, graphs, or number sentences, I explain how the tools I used fit the problem.
I know the math facts that we have learned in school.	I think about what my solution tells me about math or other topics.	I explain how the math used here is like other math I have used.
		I use math words correctly, such as saying that 6-2 is "six minus two" or "six take-away two."

Note: Text of each dimension can be written/printed on poster paper and displayed around the room so that student can constantly refer to the "criteria for success"?

88 IT'S NOT ROCKET SCIENCE!

Some people in Rabbit Heaven hang bunches of carrots from their doors for decoration. They paint these carrots with a special gold paint that preserves them from spoiling. Each jar of paint can cover 3,000 sq. cm.

How many sq. cm would you cover if you painted your carrot?
How many carrots (the same as yours) can the people in Rabbit Heaven paint from one jar?

**PLEASE USE THE SPACE BELOW TO TELL HOW YOU SOLVED THE PROBLEM.
PLEASE SHOW ALL YOUR WORK.**

extra high

width 96 cm

Top - 3 sq cm
Bottom 1 sq cm

1. The question was how many sq cm of paint it would take to cover your carrot. my plan was to use okeaig rate paper and taped it around the carrot to get how wide it was around. So I taped it around the carrot and marked the with and the highed und then I ate the sq cm and got 96 sq cm. but that was only the sides so I put the grate paper on top of the carrot and counted the number of squars that coverd the Top and got 3 sq cm the I did the same with the bottem and got 1 sq cm.

1+3+96 = 100 sq cm
bottem Top width   surfuch area

2. The questun was how many carrot like yours could you cover with 3,000 sq cm of paint? our carrots sufuce area was 100 sq cm. my plan was to divid 3,000 sq cm of paint by 100, our carrots sutace area. So I punched in on the cacylater: 3,000 divided by 100 and got 30. So we could paint 30 carrots just like ors with 3,00 cans of paint. ↓

The Carrot Project. Guided. March 28, 1994

ASSESSING STUDENT LEARNING

89

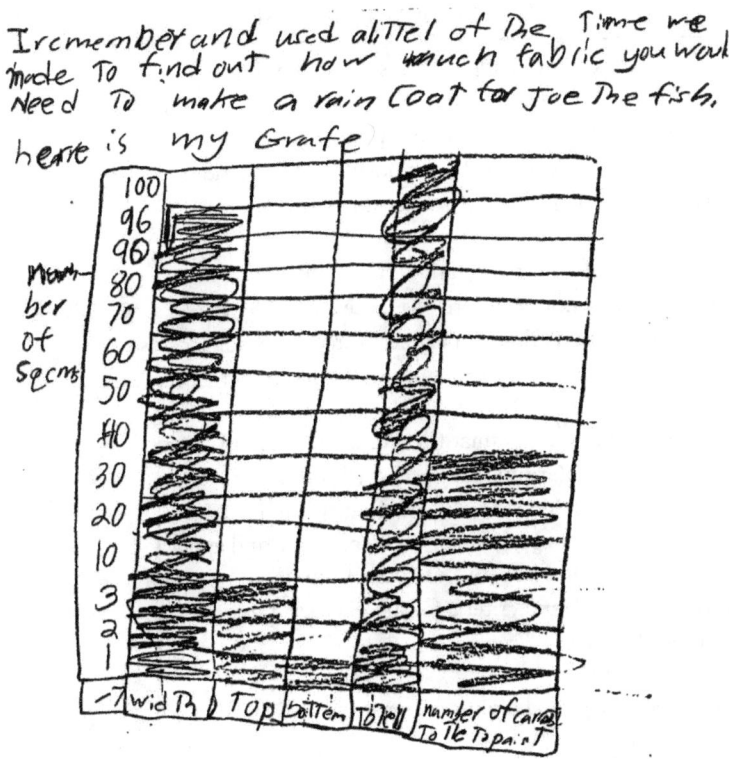

Figure 4.9. Carrot Project Student Work. After Rubric Introduction

While we fully understand that this is but one example, our experience has shown us that the more involved students are in their learning, and particularly in how they show understanding, the more engaged they are in the overall learning process.

Crafting Rubrics

For most of us, using pre-designed rubrics is easier than creating our own. Again, as professionals, beginning with a model, created by someone else, is an excellent place to start. However, if teachers wish to create their own, we list a few ideas to consider in doing so. We break down this process into PRE-task and POST-task. The pre-task (Table 4.5) includes steps to include prior to grading the work and is a means to collect ideas before you use the rubric on student work. After you develop this, it is useful to review the rubric as if you

Table 4.5. Basic Steps for Creating a Rubric—Pre-Task

1. Start Small. Attempt one type of assessment at a time.
2. Begin with an idea, usually in the form of your goals and objectives.
   - Ideas also flow from the activity to the objectives.
3. Brainstorm ways for students to demonstrate understanding.
   - Think of as many ways to attain understanding.
   - Link to criteria for performance tasks.
4. Select one type of assessment task.
   - Decide if descriptive criteria for success is appropriate.
5. Brainstorm all criteria that you believe is important for success.
   - Decide if criteria fit into dimensions if criteria and success categories are holistic.
   - Consider Response Format (Written, Oral, Group, Project).
6. Construct Task and Criteria for Success (Rubric).
   - Consider all material needed and how it is to be used.
   - Identify each category, include a description, and apply a score.
   - Provide students with student copy of rubric.
7. Clearly explain task and criteria for success to the students.
   - In the "It Depends" category.
     o Model task.
   - Provide models and discussion opportunities for Rubric Understanding.
     o Complete a Dry-Run.

Table 4.6. Basic Steps for Using and Revising the Rubric—Post-Task

1. Collect student work.
2. Read through and create piles based on initial criteria.
3. Re-evaluate each category, and possibly create new or combine existing categories.
   - For example. First Categories were.

     Excellent   Good   Fair
   - Through evaluating student work, you identify new categories*

     Excellent   Very Good   Good   Fair   Poor

   *You identified criteria that differentiated Excellent from Very Good and Fair from Poor.
   - Finally, if needed, you change the scores for each category.
     o Example: the initial rubric had three scores, the new one has five.
4. Review process with students.
   - Provide models of exemplary work.
   - Allow opportunities of self-assessment.
   - Ask for ideas for clarification.
   - Do another task.
5. Refine until students have the criteria internalized.

were actually grading an assignment. This helps to eliminate and/or include what is essential for ease of grading. The post-task analysis is done after you have actual student work and (Table 4.6) shows potential changes you might make based on their submissions.

Each type of rubric serves a different purpose and is dictated by the assignment students are completing. Being as specific as possible on the description at each level of the earned grade helps with the clarity of the work. In classrooms that incorporate rubrics on a regular basis we find students in all grades become accustomed to understanding the expectations of each assignment. Students in the primary grades also benefit from a rubric and should be taught how to effectively use a rubric to help them demonstrate their understanding. Rubrics assist students in becoming more independent in their learning and helps improve educational outcomes.

Utilizing Pre-Assessments

Throughout this chapter, we have established the significance of assessments as means for students to show understanding and detailed how we can gage learning in or *after* a lesson or unit. Fundamentally, we want to answer the question, *how do we know students have learned it?*

At times, however, we want to assess student understanding *before* teaching. Here, we possess a different assessment tool called a *pre-assessment*. Pre-assessments help teachers establish students' prior knowledge. In doing so, we can better design learning which not only incorporates what they know but also helps to embody new learning.

A pre-assessment is given initially to assess the knowledge and understanding the students already hold and is given prior to teaching the unit. Since the planning stage is mostly completed at the start of the unit, data from a pre-assessment can be used to make minor changes and then modify and/or further develop, subsequent lessons, to meet the needs of the students. Each year, depending on the group of students, and the knowledge they possess prior to teaching, there could be a shift in the focus of the lessons and depth, based on the pre-assessment.

After teaching the entire unit another assessment, post-assessment, can be designed, one with the same skills as the pre-assessment but one that offers more depth. The marked improvement shown in the later assessment provides evidence of the learning and knowledge students have acquired.

Understanding where the students are in their knowledge, through the pre-assessment, helps to fine-tune the teaching and focus of the entire unit.

Analysis of Assessment Use

Whether using a rubric, incorporating a pre-assessment, or both, the analysis of the assessments is another critical piece to informing current and future teaching. The key for any assessment is to ensure an alignment between the instruction and how students are showing learning. We mentioned earlier Bloom's long-standing frustration that most of classroom assessments still fall within the lower-level categories of the cognitive domain. Addressing higher-level thinking is difficult yet, is valuable to help craft new instruction to better serve the needs of the students. To do so, we have created a *Unit Assessment Summary Table*, whose sole purpose is to help identify *what* and *why* of the assessments, and to *determine* and *analyze* where each is linked to the categories in Bloom's (1956) Cognitive Domain. To simplify the process, we created a table to aid in the planning phases of assessment, allowing us to keep track of what the assessments are, and whether we are assessing lower or higher-order thinking (see Table 4.7). While we believe that all columns are important, columns two, three and four are most beneficial with column four leading directly to identifying where the assessments are within Bloom's (1956) domain. Table 4.8 shows a pre-service intern's summary table for the unit, *Space* and Figure 4.10 shows one on *The Chesapeake Bay*. The key for each assessment is to have something to review and analyze so that decisions can be made on what students have learned. In particular, it is important to look at the *level in Bloom* category to discern if the assessments are varied or if they tend to fall in one Bloom category more than the others.

In the process of multi-dimensional rubric analysis, it is important to keep track of how well each student does in each dimension. Some students may be excellent and show strong content knowledge but may be weaker at communicating how they solved the problem. Utilizing a simple table enables teachers to identify what their students are good at but more importantly, where they may need to improve upon. Using the TIMS Carrot Project as an example, Table 4.9 showcases how this data collection may look.

Table 4.7. Unit Assessment Summary Table

Unit Big Idea:				
Lesson Title/# Objective	Type of Assessment and When?	Why This Way? (Rationale for THIS type of assessment) Make sure the lesson aligns to objective and teaching	Level in Cognitive Domain See BLOOM	Expected Outcome *Students will . . .*
1				
2				
3				
More if needed.				

Table 4.8. Pre-Service Interns' Unit Assessment Summary Table of Space Unit

Lesson Title/# Objective	Type of Assessment and When?	Why This Way? (Rationale for THIS type of assessment) Make sure the lesson aligns to objective and teaching	Level in Cognitive Domain See BLOOM	Expected Outcome Students will ...
Pre-assessment Introduction to Space-#1 Students will be able to demonstrate their prior knowledge by filling out a KWL chart and making concept tags.	KWL Chart, Scavenger Hunt, Name Tag	We wanted to see what the students already knew about space before we got started. Then we wanted them to make name tags relating to space to get them thinking about concepts in space that we may learn later in the semester. Last, we had them do a scavenger hunt to get them out of their seats and moving while still learning new things about space.	Synthesis and Comprehension	By the end of class students will be able to construct a KWL chart by using their prior knowledge on space. Students will collect facts from scavenger hunt to discuss new ideas about space.
The Sun is a Star #2 Students will be able to construct a concept showing the characteristics of the sun.	A concept map about the sun	We wanted students to make a concept map that would include the characteristics of the sun. It would also allow them to make connections between the learned material.	Comprehension	Describe the characteristics of the sun and sketch observations.

Table 4.8. Continued

Lesson Title/# Objective	Type of Assessment and When?	Why This Way? (Rationale for THIS type of assessment)	Level in Cognitive Domain See BLOOM	Expected Outcome *Students will . . .*
Day/Night, Axis, Rotation #3 Students will be able to model how the earth rotates on an axis by making a simulation.	Observations in journal, completion of model, quiz on BrainPOP completed as whole group after video	Make sure the lesson aligns to objective and teaching We completed the quiz at the end of the video to make sure the students were paying attention to the video before we went further into the concept. Next, we had the student's model how day and night occur by modeling it using themselves as Earth, Sun, and the moon. This got the students up and moving while giving them each a role. Last, we graded their observations of the shadow tracker in order to get a better look at what they learned about how it applies to us on a real-world application.	Analysis and Application	By the end of the lesson the students will observe the rotation of the sun by watching a BrainPop Jr. video. Students will also model how the earth rotates on an axis to create day and night. Students will observe a shadow tracker to apply learning to real-world phenomena.

Unit Big Idea: The Earth and Sun in Space.

Unit Assessment Summary Table

Unit Big Idea: The Chesapeake Bay

Lesson Title/#	Type of Assessment and When?	Why This Way? (Rationale for THIS type of assessment)	Level in Cognitive Domain	Expected Outcome *Students will ...*
1. Introduction to the Chesapeake Bay	Alternative assessment Discussions	This lesson is to assess prior knowledge and introduce the topic for this unit. Formal assessment would be inappropriate.	Knowledge	Demonstrate background knowledge and begin think in terms of the Chesapeake Bay.
2. Watershed and Mapping	Completion exit ticket given at the end	The completion portion requires students to understand the terms learned that day to complete it.	Knowledge, Comprehension, Application	Define watershed and analyze the map to see what the Chesapeake Bay watershed is consisted of.
3. The Water Cycle	Alternative Assessment at the end (essay like)	Students must use the terms learned that day to write a story.	Knowledge, Comprehension, Application, and Analysis	Define the processes of the water cycle and understand that water changes from one physical state to another.
4. Estuaries and Water Salinity	Completion worksheet at the end of the lesson.	Requires students to understand definitions in order to complete tasks on the work sheet.	Knowledge, Comprehension, Application	Be able to explain the role water salinity plays in the Chesapeake bay and define estuary.
5. Pollution	Alternative Assessment at the end (essay like)	Students must know the two sources of pollution and identify the different types to complete their task.	Knowledge, Comprehension, Application.	Distinguish between point and non-point solution and identify different kinds of pollution.
6. Recycling	Short answer exit ticket.	Students must understand what items are recyclable and the benefits of recycling to complete the exit ticket.	Knowledge, Comprehension, Application	Explain which items are recyclable and what actions can be taken to recycle more in daily lives.
7. Biodiversity	Short answer exit ticket.	Students must be able to define biodiversity in their own terms.	Knowledge.	Define biodiversity and explain why being more diverse is better for the environment.
8. Ecosystems and	Matching exit ticket.	Students must use terms learned	Knowledge,	Define ecosystem and habitat and

ASSESSING STUDENT LEARNING 97

Lesson Title/#	Type of Assessment and When?	Why This Way? (Rationale for THIS type of assessment)	Level in Cognitive Domain	Expected Outcome *Students will ...*
Habitats		that day to complete the matching exercise.	Comprehension, Application	be able to distinguish between the two terms.
9. Food Chains and Food Web	Completion and matching exit ticket.	This will illustrate if students learned the terms from the lesson and is able to apply them to examples in real life.	Knowledge, Comprehension, Application, Analysis	Define herbivore, omnivore, carnivore, consumer and producer and explain their role in the food chain and food web.
10. Overharvesting	Short answer	Students must be able to use terms and information learned in the lesson to support the opinion question.	Knowledge, Comprehension, Application, Analysis	Define overharvesting and explain the effects it has on the Chesapeake Bay.
11. Review	Game and Packet with all question variety types	Students will be able to review for the test with group members and individually.	Knowledge, Comprehension, Application, Analysis	Recall information learned throughout the unit.
12. Test	Exam with all question variety types.	Students individual knowledge gained during the Chesapeake Bay Unit will be evaluated.	Knowledge, Comprehension, Application, Analysis	Recall information learned throughout the unit.

Figure 4.10. Unit Assessment Summary Table for Unit on Chesapeake Bay

Table 4.9. Multi-Dimensional Rubric Profile of Student Work

Task	Name (Partners)	4	3	2	1	Comments
Carrot Project	Sarah and	K, T, S				
	Kate	K, S	T			Need to focus on her ability to tell how she solves problems.
Carrot Project	Mike		K, T, S			

Table header spans: Use the Following Letters to Keep Track of the Dimensions / K = Knowledge, S = Solving, and T = Telling

Summary

We have examined the different categories of assessments, analyzed the components of implementing well-designed assessments, compared multiple means of assessments, and studied strategies to prepare students to be successful in this chapter. We have discussed the importance of monitoring students' understandings at different parts of the lesson through the *formative, summative* and *assessment checks*. Also, we looked at how relevant the data obtained from assessments is to impact future learning and student outcomes.

It is evident that there are many moving parts to creating effective assessments. However, it is a key component of effective curriculum design. Assessments provide teachers with the information to know if the students are truly understanding the material and to what extent they have mastered the content and skills within the learning. It is often a missed piece in a pre-service teacher's lessons, since time management during a lesson is difficult for new teachers. However, it is imperative that every lesson culminates with a *planned closure and assessment*. The *planned closure* reinforces the concepts learned and solidifies the understandings. Teachers help students make connections in this part of the lesson as they bring the objective (and/or driving question) back to the forefront to check for understanding and alignment of the learning before they complete the assessment. The assessment then provides evidence as to *How will I know they have learned it?* It should metaphorically, tie a bow on the learning and ultimately on educational outcomes.

As our work culminates in creating effective curriculum design, we would be remiss if we did not return to our five essential questions that drives our entire process.

(1) *What do I want the students to know?*
(2) *What do I want our students to do?*
(3) *Why am I teaching this?*
(4) *Why am I teaching IT this way?*
(5) *How will I know they have learned it?*

These questions provide the framework for well-structured curriculum and help to guide the challenging work that you do as teachers. As we have proven throughout our work in this manual and in our work with pre-service and veteran teachers, this systematic approach, going through deconstruction, reconstruction, planning and assessment, makes curriculum design easier and more attainable. In essence its breaks the process into manageable workable steps.

As you move into your careers, either new or growing careers, this increased knowledge on curriculum design will help you to develop and facilitate effective instruction that will impact the educational outcomes and experiences for your students.

Chapter 4: Assessment Activities

Activity One

- Using Figure 4.2 collect as many assessment ideas as you can for a unit that you want to teach.
- In what ways has using this format impacted your thinking on how you want to assess student understanding?

Activity Two

- Using the list from Activity One, create two formative assessments and describe how each will assess the main idea of that lesson.

- Create a summative assessment for a unit in which second graders read different fairy tales and learn about the components of a well-written fairy tale. Make sure the summative assessment is not a written test.
- Create a summative assessment for a unit in which fourth graders learn about the different types of bridges and what makes a bridge operate effectively. Make sure the summative assessment is not a written test.

Activity Three

- Pick one multiple means of assessment and describe how you will incorporate it into an assessment for a fourth-grade unit on Simple Machines.
- Pick a different multiple means of assessment and describe how you will incorporate it into an assessment for a second-grade unit on double-digit addition.

Activity Four

Using the TIMS Multi-dimensional Rubric and the Profile of student work chart assess all dimensions (K, S, and T) for the two student samples (Figures 4.11. and 4.12). Based on student work rationalize your scoring.

ASSESSING STUDENT LEARNING   101

Some people in Rabbit Heaven hang bunches of carrots from their doors for decoration. They paint these carrots with a special gold paint that preserves them from spoiling. Each jar of paint can cover 3,000 sq. cm.

How many carrots (the same as yours) can the people in Rabbit Heaven paint from one jar?
PLEASE USE THE SPACE BELOW TO TELL HOW YOU SOLVED THE PROBLEM.
PLEASE SHOW ALL YOUR WORK.

1. I wrap the edge of the [ruler] around the [carrot]. then divided the [carrot] up in parts. 1st part 21 sq cm, 2nd 24 sq cm, 3rd 40 sq cm, 4th 20 sq cm. Now I'll put together the odds and ends. Now I have to add up the odds and ends 13 sq cm and parts.
  21 sq cm
  24 sq cm
  40 sq cm
  20 sq cm   see back
I used the caculator 118 sq cm
The Carrot Project, March 28, 1994
to add this up   answer for how much my carrot needs

now since there is 3,000 sq cm in a jar of paint and 118 sq cm on my carrots; 3,000 ÷ 118 is
~~25.423728~~
round it off and get about 25. [carrot]

Figure 4.11. Carrot Project Student Sample Number One

_____ Date _____
_____ Grade _____

Some people in Rabbit Heaven hang bunches of carrots from their doors for decoration. They paint these carrots with a special gold paint that preserves them from spoiling. Each jar of paint can cover 3,000 sq. cm.

How many carrots (the same as yours) can the people in Rabbit Heaven paint from one jar?

PLEASE USE THE SPACE BELOW TO TELL HOW YOU SOLVED THE PROBLEM. PLEASE SHOW ALL YOUR WORK.

The ansewer is 10 carots the people of Rabbit Heaven can oly paint 10 of my carrots. I took 194 sqcm from 3,000 sqcm. This is just like the time I had to paint my desk at home. I used a graph. Calcyla for 1rist step - I used a graph to help me to find out what was the sq cm of the carrot and it was 194 sac Second step - I took 194 sq cm from 3,000 sac Third step - I got the ansewer it is 10 carrots. It was fun!!!

Figure 4.12. Carrot Project Student Sample Number Two

References

Bloom, B. S. (1956). *Taxonomy of educational objectives. Handbook: The cognitive domain.* David McKay.

Gardner, H. (1983). *Frames of mind: The theory of multiple intelligences* (1st ed.). Basic Books.

Gardner, H. (2011). *Frames of mind: The theory of multiple intelligences* (3rd ed.). Basic Books.

Hart, D. (1994). *Authentic assessment handbook: A handbook for educators.* Addison-Wesley.

Sizer, T. R. (1984). *Horace's compromise: The dilemma of the American high school.* Houghton Mifflin.

Wiggins, G., & McTighe, J. (2005). *Understanding by design* (expanded 2nd ed.). ASCD.

INDEX

Alsaleh 9, 11
Anderson 31, 50
Assessment 4, 10–11, 29, 33–34, 38, 41–42, 46, 50, 52, 55, 58, 60, 63–65, 67–68, 71–80, 82, 90–95, 97–100

Big Idea 4–7, 10–11, 13–17, 19, 21, 23, 25–27, 30, 35–38, 40–41, 49, 52, 63, 76–77, 93, 95
Bloom Revised 31
Bloom's Taxonomy of Educational Objectives 30–31, 50
Bruner 4–5, 11

Chunking/Group work 56, 58–59, 62
Coalition of Essential Schools 4
Conceptual-based curriculum planning 4
Constructivist Learning Model 4, 10, 12, 55, 63–67, 70
Content 1, 2, 5–6, 8–10, 13–17, 19–20, 22–27, 33, 35, 38–39, 41–43, 48, 51, 54–55, 64, 68, 71, 74, 76, 79, 83, 92, 98

Critical thinking 8–9, 11–12, 31–32, 42

Deconstruction 6–11, 13–23, 25–27, 30, 35–36, 44, 47, 54, 68, 71, 99
Delpit 5, 11
Dewey 4, 11, 63, 69
Driving question 1, 10, 13, 29–30, 39–42, 48, 51–52, 57–58, 64–65, 67, 71, 76–78, 98

Edwards 5, 11
Erikson 4
Essential Questions 4, 10, 29, 39–40, 49, 99

Flynn 9, 11
Formative assessment 41, 52, 58, 64–65, 72, 99

Gallagher 4, 10, 12, 55–56, 70
Gardner 69, 73, 102
Gradual Release of Responsibility (GRR) 4, 10, 55–56, 63

Instructional model 2, 4, 10, 46, 51–56, 63, 69
Interactive strategies 54, 69

Know/Do statements 10, 29, 34–35, 38, 44, 46–47
Krathwohl 31, 50

Ladson-Billings 3, 11
Lesson plan 1–2, 10, 25, 34, 40, 43, 51–53, 55–56, 63, 65–66, 68

McTighe 4, 10, 12, 29, 39–40, 50, 76–77, 101
Mercer 5, 11
Multi-dimensional rubrics 73, 82–84, 86–87, 92, 98, 100
Nisbett 9, 12

Objectives 8, 10, 29–35, 37–38, 41–50, 52, 55, 57–60, 62, 64–66, 75–79, 90, 93–95, 98, 102
Overarching concepts 5, 13
Overarching questions 41–42

Padilla 42–43, 50
Pearson 4, 10, 12, 55–56, 70
Pre-assessment 91–92, 94

Process skills 2, 5–6, 8–10, 13–17, 19–20, 23–27, 31, 33, 35, 38, 42–43, 47, 50–51, 64, 76

Quick assessment checks/all student responses 73–74

Reconstruction 9–11, 25, 29–30, 35, 37–38, 41, 44, 47, 49, 52, 54, 68, 71, 99
Rubrics 73, 76, 79–80, 82–87, 89–92, 98, 100

Scope and sequence 10, 25, 29–30, 38, 43–44, 46, 49
Sizer, Theodore 4, 10, 12, 29, 39, 50, 54, 70, 72, 102, 105
Sub-concepts 16–17, 19, 49
Summative assessment 10, 46, 72–73, 98, 100

Topical questions 41–42

Understanding by Design, UbD 4, 12, 50, 102

Wiggins, Grant 4, 10, 12, 29, 39–41, 50, 76–77, 102

Yager 1, 4, 10, 12, 63, 70

ABOUT THE AUTHORS

Robert W. Blake, Jr, is a Professor in Elementary Education and a former department chair. With a Ph.D. in Curriculum Design from the University Illinois at Chicago, a MAT in Biology from Brown University, and a Bachelor of Science in Biology from the State University of New York at Albany, Dr Blake has had 35 plus year career in science teaching as well as pre-service and in-service teacher preparation. Notable publications include a analysis of Sizer's (1984) *Horace's Compromise*, in DeVitis, Joseph L. (Ed.) (2016). *Popular educational classics: A reader; Becoming a teacher: Using Narrative as reflective practice. A cross-disciplinary approach*, edited by Blake, R.W., Jr. and Blake, B. E. (2012); *and Inside-Out: Environmental Science in the Classroom and the Field, Grades 3-8, by* Blake, R.W., Jr.; Frederick, J.A., Haines, S, and Lee, S. (2010).

Lisa R. Trattner has a Ph.D. in Educational Leadership from Notre Dame of Maryland University, a MAT In Early Childhood Education from Towson University and a Bachelor of Arts in Journalism from the University of Maryland at College Park. Dr Trattner's educational career has spanned over three decades including working as an elementary school teacher, math resource teacher and a science department chair before moving into the collegiate level. As a professor over the past 17 years, she has taught courses in curriculum design, action research, diversity, equity and inclusion, literacy and science education. She has spent much of her career at the college level working directly with pre-service teachers in the field and mentoring new teachers as they transition into their teaching careers. Publications include *The Complexities of a Nineteenth Century Icon: Emma Hart Willard*, 2021 and "Making Science Come Alive," 2015.

Critical Literacies and Language: Pedagogies of Social Justice

Lead Editor
Brett Elizabeth Blake

Editor
Judith M. Dunkerly

One of the most fundamental aspects of a just society is the right to create equitable and inclusive spaces of belonging for all people while also confronting injustice and oppression. However, we are now in a time where seeking justice and equity is met with neoliberalism, which pervades the academy at all levels of education. Yet, for many, this is not a time for retreat, but rather a moment of solidarity, a time to create new knowledge and understanding through struggle. As Freire wrote, "Knowledge emerges only through invention and re-invention, through the restless, impatient, continuing, hopeful inquiry human beings pursue in the world, with the world, and with each other." Thus, the purpose of this series is to provide literacy and language researchers, practitioners, as well as community activists, with a space to actualize and embody a restless, impatient never-finished objective of critical literacies and language education. It is the aim of this series to create a space to share research that promotes pedagogies of equity. We also recognize that different audiences have different needs. To that end, we seek to provide, when applicable, a "notebook" as a companion to research volumes to facilitate actionable steps for the PK-12 classroom or community spaces. This series is different as it approaches the dissemination of critical work from a place of intentionality to address the gap in disseminating research (typically read by scholars) and the need to have it "on the ground" for classroom teachers, community activists, and workers. By creating companion volumes (where applicable), there is a greater chance for sustained criticality in literacy education.

For additional information about this series or for the submission of manuscripts, please contact:

    Brett Elizabeth Blake, General Editor
    blakeb@stjohns.edu

To order other books in this series, please contact our Customer Service Department:

    peterlang@presswarehouse.com (within the U.S.)
    orders@peterlang.com (outside the U.S.)

Or browse online by series:

    www.peterlang.com

www.ingramcontent.com/pod-product-compliance
Lightning Source LLC
Chambersburg PA
CBHW061719300426
44115CB00014B/2757